An OUTLAW in MY HEART

A POLITICAL ACTIVIST'S USER'S MANUAL

STEPHEN GASKIN

Camino Books, Inc.

Philadelphia

Manufactured in the United States of America

1 2 3 4 5   03 02 01 00

Library of Congress Cataloging-in-Publication Data

Gaskin, Stephen.
   An outlaw in my heart : a political activist's user's manual / Stephen Gaskin.
      p. cm.
   Includes bibliographical references.
   Contents: A hippie in the White House. Why I'm running for president.
   Platform. Campaign statement. Free thought and the Constitution. We forget
   who we are. An open letter. Other presidential candidates, presidents—
   A reader. Being a hippie. Campaign finance and political office reforms.
   Corporations. Universal health care and education. Cannabis. Women.
   Animal rights. Gay rights. Family. Environment. Gun control. Yard goods—
   The last word.
      ISBN 0-940159-64-3 (alk. paper)
      1. United States—Politics and government—1993– 2. United States—
   Social conditions—1980– 3. Gaskin, Stephen—Political and social views.
   4. Greens/Green Party USA. 5. Presidents—United States—Election—2000.
   I. Title.

E889.G37 2000
973.929—dc21   00-010225

Cover and interior design: Jerilyn Kauffman

This book is available at a special discount on bulk purchases for promotional, business, and educational use. For information write to:

Publisher
Camino Books, Inc.
P.O. Box 59026
Philadelphia, PA 19102

www.caminobooks.com

Also by Stephen Gaskin

40 Miles of Bad Road

Monday Night Class

The Caravan

Hey Beatnik! This Is the Farm Book

This Season's People

Volume One: Sunday Morning Services on the Farm

Mind at Play

Amazing Dope Tales and Haight Street Flashbacks

Rendered Infamous

Cannabis Spirituality

What is going to carry us through is faith and love and good principles. Faith that there are such things as love and good principles, and the nerve to try to use them and carry them out.

We should ask for the sake of all mankind that there be peace and that there be understanding and that true grace come onto us to help us get this planet together, because this planet needs to get together.

—*This Season's People*, p. 167

Contents

Foreword

One of the things about living a long time is that you get to see stuff repeated often enough that you start seeing the pattern to it. I've lived long enough to see some patterns in our country that sadden me.

One of the patterns is that we've lost our social consciousness. We sue one another and talk about our God-given rights rather than our personal and social responsibilities. A San Francisco punk band did a version of the old song suggesting that "Everybody get together and love one another right now." It was so badly out of tune, so screwed, so sarcastic, so ironic, and so nasty it about made you want to barf. And that was their point. They were saying about these times: "Can you still sing that sucker?" Their remake was hard to listen to, but you had to admit that there was a certain amount of justice in it.

Another pattern is that we're losing our freedoms because "special powers" are granted during emergency crises—and these special powers are never given back. That's what Hitler did, and that's how he consolidated his power. And that's how the fix we're in now has come about in great measure: special powers are being taken for special things.

Somewhere along the line, I think possibly caused in the beginning by the effort against Germany in World War II, came the "win at all costs" thing that we believed we had to buy into.

So we actually devised a nuclear bomb and used it.

And we began incorporating into our own policies the evil we faced.

We've got to get down to walking the walk as well as talking the talk in this country.

It shames me intensely whenever there is a big international meeting about how we're not going to whale anymore, how we're not going to have land mines anymore, how we're going to boycott Nestlé's, how we're going to do what we can to conserve energy. . . and the United States is the only holdout every time.

The place where the world is right now requires that you must come out and fight—because we live in a world where human beings are bought and sold. So I've decided to run for President, and I'm coming from the old traditional place where Eugene V. Debs took his stand: "As long as there is a lower class, I am of it. As long as people are in prison for their political beliefs, I am not free."

Nobody's talking for that.

Well, I am.

I don't think, though, that a candidate is supposed to go around trying to find out what people want and then tell them they're supposed to get it.

Being in political office shouldn't be thought of or perceived as just being about what one can do for others. The electorate should also be thinking of what they should do for someone else, not just what should be done for them. They should start having a little social awareness. It comes back to old religious teaching: What thy eye should see to do, turn thy hand to and do it.

I'm an independent Yankee, and I believe in the Constitution. The Constitution exists to assure that the big ones just don't eat all the little ones. It's a noble ideal, and it's always going to be infringed on by the folks who want to rig the machine to be sure they don't lose.

I have no illusions about winning the election to become the President of the United States. While I had hoped to run as the candidate for the Green Party, Ralph Nader recently won that party's nomination. Now, I am running on my own for my Outlaw Party. What I always say, though, is that if you think you're going to lose anyway, why don't you stick with the real ideals?

So I'm going to share with you my real ideals.

But I have to say ahead of time that I experience censorship. The kind of thing I can talk about is severely restricted. It is assumed that I have a specialty, which is being a hippy. I experience censorship regularly on that basis; and I know that anyone else in a position similar to mine also experiences that same censorship. The news that goes out on television for half an hour has to be combed and filtered and winnowed down and siphoned off and evaporated until it is such a thin mixture and so little, compared to the number of things that actually went on that day, as to give a simplistic view of the world.

It's very difficult to know what is really going on. It requires effort on your part, or you aren't going to know what's going on. I know this because I know something that most people in this country don't yet know, but I will tell you: the government lies.

I love my country, but I'm sometimes ashamed of my government. . . and I don't think I'm alone in this. I'm running for President because, in whatever way I can, I want to end that shame.

PART I

A Hippy
in the White House

Stephen and grandfriend E.J. Dixon.

CHAPTER 1

Why I Want to Be President

I want to be President because the country that I've lived in for 65 years is not as free as it was when I was born, and it's gotten less free all my life. I still believe in the Constitution that I learned about in the third grade, and I would like to see that be what we live under, and not this patched-together thing that the corporations have bought.

The large corporations are in the business of buying the world. Once they've bought it, they will do what they please, and it's up to the American government to stop them because they are the only force that is big enough to do that. America is the only country that has a large enough and rich enough electorate to cause our government to listen to us at all.

The corporations have no business forming a world trade organization. The governments of the world need to get together and make trade agreements for the people, and regulate world trade for the benefit of all the people of the world. If I were President, I would make the corporations operate in the public interest, and would pass laws stopping the big mergers and forcing corporations to act in the best interest of the people and the planet.

The thing is, the biosphere is one living organism and it is deathly sick. We are killing miles and miles of it by the day, and we have not caught on yet. We can pass high-sounding resolutions, but when it comes down to it, the corporations that own the forests get to cut them and burn them if they want to. This sort of thing has got to stop.

I want to run because I want to send a message to the Democrats and the Republicans that they are not the only parties out

there and they do not represent a large part of the American people. With my campaign, I want to show that somebody without
any money and without being backed up by any corporations can
go out and on the truth of ideas, try to give heart to the youth to
let them understand that it is not totally lost; it's still up for grabs,
and there's a lot they can do.

We have to get the politicians to start talking about the real issues that are tearing up people's lives, and be big enough and vo-
cal enough to get some real commitments from them about clean-
ing up the environment, clearing out our prisons, and making it
possible for people to have real freedom in this country, like we're
supposed to be guaranteed under the Constitution.

Remember those bought and paid-for scientists who have
been explaining the weather away for the sake of business? The
Republicans got a bunch of medium-weight college guys who
would say (for money) that global warming was a myth. Remember the one who said, "It will be warmer, you'll like it." These
were the guys who said that business would be harmed by trying
to do something about the problem. I think those guys should step
forward and explain themselves to the people in north Florida
who saw the wetlands burn from El Niño–related weather, and to
the people whose homes have been washed away from Korea to
Malibu to the Midwest.

Our own business interests lie to us for money on our airwaves all the time. By now everybody knows that tobacco will kill
you. Honest legislators on state and federal levels worked for
years to bring big tobacco to accountability. The tobacco companies spent 40 million dollars on ads and who knows how much on
individual legislators, and suddenly they weren't in trouble.

That is the kind of thing that almost brings me to tears every
day. Here's another one. All the countries of the world got together and tried to make agreements about reducing global warming. Experts showed the problem and everyone voted to do something about it, except the United States, which is the biggest
polluter. Our Republican Congress wouldn't act.

Here's another one. All the countries of the world got together
and tried to make agreements about reducing infant mortality by
encouraging breastfeeding instead of allowing hospitals to force

Nestlé's formula packs on new mothers in Third World countries where refrigeration is not in common use. Everyone voted to do something about it, except the United States, which took Nestlé's side against all the experts.

At the same time that it is painfully clear that all of our foreign and domestic policy depends on and is run by money, we as a society and country have the nerve to set ourselves up to be the judge of the world in every religious and moral question.

The medical interests and the HMOs are trying to have pregnancy, birth, and menopause declared to be diseases to continue with their policy of making money off of every human event.

The war on drugs as it's being played out in the U.S. these days is a concerted, organized attack on a minority of the population that would itself be a small country—maybe 25, 35, or 40 million people. The Constitution is being damaged severely by this; we're losing all the protections from government abuse and we're turning into a police state. The man we have made our drug czar can not only countermand U.S. Customs regulations about what can be imported, he can start wars with other countries and send troops into other countries. We have more troops in Colombia than we had in Vietnam in the mid-'60s.

The war on drugs is not the issue itself, but it's a symptom of the general unresponsiveness and "bought-outness" of our government. It shows this government is not of the people, by the people, and for the people, which Proposition 215 proves. People in California have been arrested and given a hard time for abiding by Proposition 215, which was a medical marijuana use referendum passed by the electorate, and if there's anything holy in democracy it ought to be a referendum passed by the electorate.

There's hardly any Left in this country anymore, unless you count the marijuana legalization movement. This movement is one of the most authentic progressive campaigns that can now be found, a group of concerned people from all cultures bound together by their belief that the laws against marijuana are unreasonable to the point of insanity. These hundreds of thousands of people are affected by the drug war in the same way that the youth of the country were once affected by Vietnam. In those days, everybody knew somebody who'd been drafted, was going to Vietnam, or had been killed or injured. Now everybody knows somebody who's on trial, going to jail on mandatory minimums, or maybe even doing life.

That brings me to the young new voters out there. The only voting pool that I know of with enough people who are idealistic enough to make actual changes in the political landscape are the youth. And I want them to come out and make Richard Nixon sorry he gave them the vote. I want them to come out and turn the world around because they are the only force that can do it. I want them to say to America, "We're not consumers; we are the people for whom the world was made, and for whom it should be run."

I want the youth to come out massively, and I want them to vote for alternative candidates, like me, or alternative parties, like the Green Party. My platform is about as forward-thinking, as inclusive, as fair and as good a starting place as you'll find for turning this thing around. So my message to young people of voting age is register to vote, register Green, and educate yourself.

We, the inheritors of the country and the world, now have our turn to band together peacefully in public, register to vote, and make politicians pay attention to what we are saying. This is our right, and it is our obligation.

That's why it's so important to get alternative parties on the ballot in as many states as possible. We have to let the Democrats and the Republicans know that they are not the only game in town, and that there's a much better game being played over on the other side of the fence. I'm hoping that my presence in a presidential race can attract first-time voters, disillusioned political dropouts, and a bunch of other people who can help make a big noise in an election.

CHAPTER 2

Platform

My campaign emphasizes the following planks:

Plank 1: Campaign Finance and Election Reform.

The airwaves belong to the people, and everybody gets a say.

The people need to have choices in their political system that allow for broader representation and full citizen participation. Proportional representation is one way that's been pretty successful in Europe in giving people a share of the say-so in return for whatever vote they cast.

Campaign spending needs to be capped, political action committees and lobbying groups need to be controlled, and the networks need to give up enough time for the people to run their elections without cost.

Plank 2: A Corporation Is Not a Person.

People are more important than profits.

It's obvious that we have to start regulating the unreasonable power and resources wielded by corporate interests. There's a bad piece of policy out there that allows a corporation the same rights as a person, and guarantees its freedom of speech to be exercised through its money. Runaway corporations are a big part of the reason why we barely have a middle class anymore—it's pretty much Bill Gates or welfare. I think big national chain stores need to sell stuff made by locals as cheaply as they sell the stuff made in Taiwan, and start giving artists, craftspeople, and small entrepreneurs a chance. We don't need more dead-end jobs, we need more opportunities for people to support themselves by their honest talents and labor, and we need the big corporations to stop gobbling up all the markets and all the resources and putting everybody to work for them.

Plank 3: Universal Health Care.

Everyone gets taken care of while we argue about the money.

In this rich country, we should immediately start treating everyone, and planning on how to share the expense fairly as we proceed. Health care must be taken away from the drug-industrial complex and returned to people, practitioners, and consumers. Alternative treatments, which give greater responsibility to individuals for their own health, must be promoted. I believe the crisis in individual health is related to the critical state of health of our planet. The environmental damage suffered by the planet is reflected in every living thing that draws its life from that same planet.

There's got to be non-profit, national health insurance. . . that comes right from the federal government, which is the cheapest way it can be done. . . not the insurance companies. Let the insurance companies insure cars and houses. . . let 'em insure Jennifer Lopez's booty. . . but just not health care.

Plank 4: Choice in Education.

Let's educate the kids now, through junior college on merit, and argue about the money later.

With all the money we save on elections, we can finally start educating our kids for the 21st century. Technology needs to be available to every kid that has an interest, whether they live in a government housing project or Indian reservation, or a middle-class suburb. If people want to educate their children at home, we need to support them to do the best job they can. If 10, 12, or 20 families want to get together and create a neighborhood school, then they should get the funding and the advising and the materials to help them do that. We need to be teaching conflict resolution and emotional literacy in all classrooms, and helping children to explore and accept the different ways of being in the world so that we can start producing more balanced, more satisfied human beings.

Plank 5: Decriminalize Marijuana and Give Amnesty to All Marijuana Prisoners Who Are Not Involved with Guns or Violence.

As part of a total system of justice reform, we must address the half-million "dissidents" imprisoned for the victimless crime of simple marijuana possession. We need to immediately decriminalize marijuana possession and release these prisoners, granting them amnesty and full return of their Constitutional rights. These folks can then vote for things like repeal of mandatory drug testing, expanded treatment and counseling, prison education and job training, repeal of the death penalty, and a bunch of other changes that need to happen in this area. There are 8 million people in the world's jails; 2 million of them are in the U.S.A. We have 4 percent of the world's population and 25 percent of the world's incarcerated. We cannot in good conscience be referred to as the land of the free.

Plank 6: Fix Veterans Benefit System.

When people go off and fight for their country, risk their lives and maybe get a little messed up in the process, then their country needs to make sure they're taken care of when they get back. Vets shouldn't have to struggle to get their benefits. The G.I. Bill should provide full educational benefits, medical care, alternative employment, and counseling, and rehabilitation should be a priority for all veterans.

Plank 7: Equal Rights Amendment for Women.

We gave women the vote, now let's give them the benefits.

It's hard for me to believe in this day and time that women do not automatically receive full, fair, and equal treatment under the law. And it's unthinkable for this kind of gender discrimination to continue. Women—and their children—are the future of the planet, and we need to start treating them with the respect and devotion they deserve. Women not only have to receive the same privileges and opportunities as men, but they also must receive greater support for their roles as mothers. There have to be more liberal policies for sick leave, vacation time, on-site daycare, and time-sharing to give women the maximum support in caring for their children. Motherhood is a positive, productive administrative service provided to the human race; it needs to be recognized as such, compensated as such, and supported by everyone else on the planet.

Plank 8: Animal Rights.

We need to recognize and protect all sentient beings.

Plank 9: Gay Rights.

The Constitution needs to be amended to apply to all people, whatever it takes, including a federal hate crimes law.

Plank 10: Quit Building and Selling War Weapons.

CHAPTER 3

Campaign Statement

It is time to take a new look at our society and to see if it still stands for what it once did. We have to redeem it and then fix it. If ignorance and greed and racism continue to force the direction of the country, we could plunge into a decadence so deep that we might not see real freedom return for a generation, if at all.

What Martin Luther King meant by "live out the meaning of our creed" was that even though the United States was originally designed for the freedom of certain kinds of white male Protestants, we know that in all decency, it should include women, people of color, and all religions.

When the Democrats have the power, they pass laws that at least claim to be for the sake of the common people, whether they end up that way or not. When the Republicans are in power, they try to recover the ground for the rich. The fight becomes more important than the well-being of the people, and the truth of the laws, which the people have to live by, is lost in the ideological wrangling.

We are asked to believe that having insurance companies suck billions of dollars out of the health care system doesn't make it more expensive.

We are asked to believe that the videotape of Rodney King being beaten by the police is not clear evidence of police brutality and racism.

We are told that nicotine is not addictive, that selling guns doesn't escalate violence, and that justice is not for sale in spite of the clear evidence of millionaires walking away untouched from capital crimes.

Doctors tell us that we have "the best health care system in the world," even though our medical system is one of the most unfair and most expensive in the western world and leaves 47 million people uncovered.

We are told that poverty and other social circumstances have nothing to do with the crime rate and that it is just coincidental that one in three young black men goes to jail.

We are told that marijuana causes violence, that it is addictive, that it has no medical or economic uses, and that it causes brain damage, impotence, and enlarged breasts in men.

We are told that the prohibition against cannabis is because of its extreme danger, even though it has been proven safer than aspirin and less addictive than coffee. Nixon's own commission returned the verdict that cannabis was the safest active substance in the pharmacopoeia.

We have changed nearly 180 degrees from our original revolutionary outlook. The U.S. has the most people in prison of any country in the "free" world. Building prisons is one of the biggest growth industries. Half a million people are in jail for marijuana offenses. People are given 20, 30, even 50 years of prison time for having or selling cannabis—more time than for murder or rape.

The idea that we are engaged in a cultural war has been preached by the far Right. They say that the troubles of the United States started in the 1960s and were all caused by the hippies.

This is another of the big untruths. The '60s were one of this country's finest hours. People like us have accomplished many of the changes that have been wrought in this country. In great measure, it was hippies and beatniks who went into the South and told Southerners that the outright segregation that they had going on was not cool. We helped get the U.S. out of Vietnam. We helped topple Nixon.

We helped educate about nukes. We helped pioneer attention to the environment and endangered species. We aided and supported native peoples, both in the U.S. and overseas. I am proud of our hippy heritage.

It is with this information and this background that I come to a conclusion that gives me no satisfaction.

There are probably 25 million marijuana smokers in the U.S. alone, as well as millions more who, if not smokers now, are still sentimental about it. The government anti-pot campaign is for the purpose of keeping these millions of people off balance to minimize their political power. All those 500,000 pot smokers doing time are out of the political process, present but not able to vote. A lot of these people are hippies and if they could vote, they would be voting for the kinds of changes that are needed in our society. They are casting their own kind of vote right now, with the sacrifice of their time, their families, and their lives in a demonstration of just how wrong and how wasteful this aspect of America's drug war really is.

The effective silencing of all those hippy voices must end now if our country is going to pull itself together and ensure real democratic freedom for all its citizens. We are getting more and more agreement that there needs to be a new ethic in this country, and I believe it's time we pull out the old hippy ethic, dust it off, and see what we can do with it.

The hippy ethic includes eating healthy, living simply, walking lightly on the earth, treating everybody like family, and taking care of the mothers and babies. I believe these are the things we need to get back to doing.

I cannot understand why war is made on these people when marijuana is not the problem. Cocaine and heroin are causes of great social damage. No one robs liquor stores or turns tricks to buy pot. That is done to buy hard drugs. People don't do desperate things for pot because it isn't addictive. Sometimes I think it's just safer for the law to pick on hippies than heavily armed Mafia or cartel drug lords.

I have come to the idea of running for President, in part, so that I can put the subject of reefer law on the table and make the debate public. I think I can be as much of a pain in the rear as Ross Perot, but for a better cause.

CHAPTER 4

Free Thought and
the Constitution

I believe in the Constitution. I think that it is one of the most important documents in history. I think it protects freedom of religion for all Americans and freedom from religion, too.

I am an American. Parts of my family have been here since 1783. There has been somebody from our family in most of the wars that this country has fought. My uncle was decorated for valor at Pearl Harbor. I am a Marine Corps combat veteran of the Korean War myself.

I used to play four-generation dominos down in Texas with my great-grandfather, my grandfather, and my mother.

My great-grandfather was born in 1850 and was a drummer boy in the Union home guard during the Civil War. He was a U.S. Marshal in the Oklahoma Indian Territory, a surveyor in the deep South, and a prospector in the far West. He was also a freethinker and a student of the world's religions.

My grandmother, who drove a covered wagon from Tennessee to Texas, was a freethinker and a suffragette who marched in the streets for the women's vote. Her brother, my great-uncle Charles, was a freethinker, too. He helped organize the longshoremen's union on the waterfront in San Francisco in the 1930s and '40s.

My mother was a freethinker, and so was my father, until he died five years ago at age 94. On his deathbed, my father made my mother promise that she wouldn't let anyone pray over him after he died. Whenever the weather is cold, my mother says, "Brr, it's cold as Christian charity."

We have been freethinkers for generations. And, as is provided for in the Constitution, I have passed my philosophical and religious ways on to my children, who are very proud of their heritage and ancestors.

I am not a backslider who needs to be roped and tied and turned back in with the rest of the herd. I come from a long and proud American tradition that includes the likes of Benjamin Franklin and Thomas Paine and Thomas Jefferson and Helen Keller and Lena Horne and Henry David Thoreau and Samuel Clemens and Herman Melville.

I think the importance of the United States lies in the sincere attempt to live without royalty and with respect for other people's religions. When I hear someone say that the separation of church and state is a myth, or that the Constitution is only man's law, it makes my blood run cold. I consider any attempt to take this country over in the name of any religion to be as repugnant and unconstitutional as a takeover by international fascism.

Stephen and Hassan Fathey at Right Livelihood Award in Stockholm, 1980.

CHAPTER 5

Service

There is a great mass of mythology connected with the turn of the millennium, the year 2000, but fortunately it is only in the Christian calendar. The whole question becomes much easier to handle if you look at it as the Year of the Dragon as in the Chinese calendar, or 5760 in the Hebrew calendar, or 6241 in the Egyptian calendar, or even 8 Cauac as in the Mayan calendar. In this way it becomes just another year and the question is not about a cycle of time that exists outside of us but about a cycle of life that exists inside of us. Then the question becomes what is our responsibility, not what will happen.

I am a believer in free will. I am not a believer in predestination. I think a belief in prophecy robs us of our free will. If you insist in wanting to know that it all comes out all right, you must give up your freedom to affect the outcome and help make it all come out all right.

Now, some people may think that I am not as religious as I used to be and it is true that on Mondays, Wednesdays, and Fridays I might be an agnostic, and on Tuesdays and Thursdays a primitive animist, while partying down on Saturdays and sometimes sitting zazen on Sunday. At no time do I subscribe to any "brand-name" religions.

I love the ethical teachings of almost all the religions and I love the psychedelic testimony of their saints. I do not believe in any of their dogmas.

I think each one of us has a non-shirkable obligation to figure out the world on our own as best we can. The way we behave as a result of that investigation is our real and practiced religion.

I consider myself to be an "ethnic" hippy. I know that the hippies were preceded by the beatniks, the bohemians, the nihilists, Voltaire, and so on back to Socrates, but the wave of the revolution that spoke to me was the hippies. Rock and roll lights my soul and gives a beat to the revolution.

When I was a child I used to hope for calamities because the world seemed so sewed up and frozen in the status quo. I longed for an earthquake or a blizzard so the world would be malleable. When I became a hippy my fondest dreams had come true. The world was up for grabs. In the following 20 or 30 years the Republicans and other forces of evil tried their level best to nail it back down.

Last election, Bill Clinton proved that the world is still up for grabs. Thank God. (You should pardon the expression.)

This brings us to here and now. Although this election will change the face of the world, it in no way excuses us from our best efforts. The New Age does not come automatically. It's like when the Arkansas traveler asked the farmer how his potatoes turned out. The farmer said, "They didn't turn out at all, me and Sal had to dig 'em out."

To me, a great deal of the "New Age" is a waste of time. Much of it seems to pander to self-interest and is material rather than spiritual. It's about "smelling this," "hearing this," "touching this," "seeing this," and "tasting this." There are more important things. How long has it been since you heard people speak of the future in terms of "great pure effort"? That Ross Perot could pull 18 million votes with the idea of "shared sacrifice" shows that people instinctively understand that service is called for.

The key to the future is service. Part of what made Kennedy great was the idea of the Peace Corps. Part of Clinton's votes came from people who liked the idea of repaying student loans with service. As the world becomes more crowded, each way of making money becomes precious and money is charged for things that used to be given for free or for love. Service becomes a revolutionary act. It must again become respectable to be an idealist.

My new project is called "Rocinante" after Don Quixote's horse, a vehicle for an incurable idealist. We are embarking on the creation of a project that will include a birth center with a midwifery training facility and a complete senior community living center, ranging from assisted living and adult daycare to a skilled care facility and a hospice for the dying. We believe that we have the experience necessary to design an inexpensive and graceful paradigm that can serve as a model for health care for the next century.

This is the wild part. As soon as I let out word of what I was doing, people wrote me from all over the United States, many of them not just interested in living at the Rocinante Center, but ones who wanted to confer on doing similar projects where they live. It is the Zeitgeist. It is the future growing from the compost of the present.

Stephen and Dennis Peron, 25th anniversary of the Human Be-In.

CHAPTER 6

We Forget Who We Are

We forget who we are. This is wrong. We must never forget that we are the people who thumbed our noses at royalty and have made it stick for over 200 years. That is what makes America important, not the gross national product.

We seem to be in a kind of political entropy. This is not just to say that everything is going to hell. Things are truly up for grabs as well. There are also great chances for advancement, but not without work.

This country was formed in one great cataclysm of revolution and began with a clear enough public self-concept that people actually geared up for a great social effort and made great personal sacrifices to change the paradigm.

As time goes on, the original concept was tested by greed, self-interest, and reality. Laws are changed and amended at the behest of lobbyists for special financial interests, sometimes to close loopholes and sometimes to open them, and the law becomes cluttered with legal fictions that become calcified into the code and are, legally, treated as truth.

If a lawmaker wants to up the ante on marijuana smokers, he can propose a law that puts marijuana in the same category with heroin. This is scientifically untrue but has been made legally "true" in almost all jurisdictions. These lies of convenience obscure truth and add to the cultural burden of untruth that weighs down our society. It obscures our national identity.

We are told that the unresponsiveness of the government, of which the extreme sanctions against cannabis are only a part so draconian as to effectively repeal the Constitutional safeguards, is to protect the public and the country, much like burning a Vietnamese village to save it. The prosecutors are instructed to get the people that are under suspicion to make a plea-bargain to save the expense of a jury trial.

This is to protect the judge and the court from any legal repercussions for playing fast and loose with your rights. The entire weight and thrust of all this legal chicanery is to give the prosecutors tools to force you to turn in your friends. It is intimidation by bludgeon. The reason that they think all this stuff is OK is because marijuana is so evil and by extension that *you* are so evil that it doesn't matter what is done to you. This is exactly the kind of crap that the Constitution was designed to protect us from. This is also why the religious Right has no real respect for the Constitution.

When the crime is so minor—having marijuana—and the punishment is so unreasonable—taking people's homes and years of their lives as well as a very real modern-day shunning—one is forced to look for deeper motives.

I have come to believe that it is not the proscription of a substance but the systematic oppression of a certain kind of people. As Jello Biafra of the Dead Kennedys said, the war on drugs is ethnic cleansing, American-style. There have been a whole series of decisions made, on local, state, and federal levels, to the effect that hippies (by which is meant anyone with committed liberal opinions) are undesirable and are to be banned, interdicted, harassed, discouraged, arrested, and pee-tested. It is a blatant use of police power to frighten and intimidate millions of people into giving up a heartfelt spiritual practice and lifestyle.

The urine test is the loyalty oath of these times. The hippies are this season's Jews, this season's Reds, and the Republican Right are this season's Joe McCarthys.

I think Perot's 18 million add up to about half the number of hippies in the United States. I want to demonstrate that our constituency is large and intelligent and worthy of consideration. People from several states have said that they would work for me in their areas. In the first place, my presidential candidacy will not even try to compete financially. That would be the first trap. I am going to rely on my good hippy karma. I am quite well known among hippies and the youth. I am also going to rely on the truth and sanity of my positions. I have been crisscrossing this continent for 28 years. My books have sold about half a million copies, and books related to my work have sold several millions. Rather than plugging time on the air, I will try to be a good enough story to be carried as news. I will be using the Internet and Web pages, and I hope to have the help of the people. We have been building a system for years. On my road trips, I usually talk on the local public access station and I have friends on that circuit from coast to coast.

I intend to put my questions on the table. I want all candidates for all offices to be asked what have they done for reefer sanity in the U.S.A. I want it to be understood that we *are* a bunch of tree huggers and mystics and greens and that there are about 35 million of us. I want to get them registered. I want us to influence the future of this nation.

> All babies together, every one a seed.
> Half of us are satisfied, half of us in need.
> And love's bountiful in us, tarnished by our greed,
> Oh, when will there be a harvest for the world?
> A nation planted, so concerned with gain,
> As the seasons come and go, greater grows the pain,
> Far too many feeling the strain.
> Oh, when will there be a harvest for the world?
> Gather every man, gather every woman,
> Open up your hearts, give thanks for the children.
> Gather everyone, gather altogether,
> Open up your love, hoping life is better
> For the world.
> Dress me up for battle when all I want is peace,
> Those of us who pay the price, come home with the least.
> And nation after nation, turning in deceit,
> Oh, when will there be a harvest for the world?

CHAPTER 7

An Open Letter

I was asked to write a little statement to students at the University of Florida who had asked me, "What in your campaign is going to help me?" I wrestled with that for a while, wrote something half-assed, and then decided to write something else. I decided to write and tell them, "I ain't really thinking about benefiting you guys except for saving your voting rights and things like that. But you guys are the beneficiaries of the system."

Greetings to all you Florida college people.

I take some issue with the form of the question. In the first place you are only going to be in college for a small part of your life. In the second, I don't think a candidate looks for certain groups and then tries to give them what they want. I am not going to promise free tuition or HDTV in every room.

What I am going to work on is campaign finance reform to get money out of politics. This is for you so when you vote it might actually mean something instead of just being a media-stimulated response that was planned and designed in some political laboratory.

I am also working for Not-for-Profit Universal National Health Insurance. If your parents are paying for your health insurance, you might not see this, but you will have to face it someday. 47 million Americans have no health care.

These kinds of things are for ALL Americans, young and old.

I want to stop the drug war, which is a war of America against its own children.

I am a 65-year-old hippy and I have been an activist for 35 years. I fear more for American freedom now than I ever have before. The grownups are screwing it and I want you to make something of yourselves and cooperate to fix the mess before it is too late.

Stephen interviewed at Million Marijuana March, 1998.

CHAPTER 8

Candidates, Presidents, and Politicians

Al Gore

I've known Al Gore for 25 years or more. He was a reporter for the *National Tennessean*, who did the first in-depth story on the Farm. . . a big, multi-page story in the newspaper on us. And we knew him for years and years. When he went for Congress, he replaced a guy we didn't like very well, and we were happy to have him. And as a senator, we liked him because he worked hard on the missile thing, worked on that kind of stuff. But I noticed that we were getting more and more remote from him.

—Television interview, THC (The Hemp Channel, Seattle, WA), Vivan McPeak, host, 1999

• • •

There's a couple of differences [between Al and me]. One of them is that I don't have any money at all, and Al Gore's family has Occidental Oil Company stock, and currently they're killing Indians in Colombia with McCaffery-dope-war-trained Colombian troops so Occidental Oil can drill on traditional land in the rain forest.

And Al knows that. He's gotta know that! He's got half a million dollars' worth of their stock. . . his father used to sit on the Occidental Board when Armand Hammer ran it.

That, to me, shows that in the long run, Al owes more to his class than he does to the people. And what we're having here in the United States is a class war. That's what I alluded to when I talked about the Left all being knocked off balance by the drug wars.

Al was one of the main guys defending the continent of Africa against being able to have their own generic drug factories so they could fight their AIDS epidemic without having to go through the big American drug companies. Al's in on that, and I'm bitterly disappointed in Al because of that stuff.

—Television interview, THC (The Hemp Channel,
Seattle, WA), Vivan McPeak, host, 1999

• • •

People ask, "Aren't you afraid that George W. is going to win because you didn't vote for Al?"

I'm gonna say, "If Al didn't have enough sense to get my vote, that's his own damn fault. I was predisposed toward him, have known him for a long time, used to think he was an honest man. And he's managed to not get my vote. He ought to notice that."

• • •

Al's excuse for the half-million dollars of Occidental stock is, "Well, that's just a trust fund my father left my mother. . . and what's wrong with that?"

Well, what's wrong with that is you didn't sell it and buy some different stock when you found out that it's drilling on traditional Indian land in the rain forest.

What's wrong with that?

• • •

One thing about Al, nobody can say that he is a traitor to his class.

• • •

In Kansas you can't teach evolution. . . and Al Gore waffled on
that question when he was asked about it.

John McCain

Like other people, I see some attractive things in McCain. But he
has one seriously fatal flaw. He's a Republican.

> —Television interview, THC (The Hemp Channel,
> Seattle, WA), Vivian McPeak, host, 1999

George W. Bush

I think Molly Ivins said that Dubya was born on third base and
thought he hit a triple.

He's not very smart, and he's pretty expedient, and he's not
very good. He thought that he was "in" because he had the name,
and was going to work a little hereditary American royalty there if
he could.

He would be a disaster because he has no real scruples and no
real ideals. He's not even a Republican ideologue. He is like
Ronald Reagan, for sale to the highest bidder, except that he can't
read his lines as well. They thought they had a hot one bought.

> —Television interview, THC (The Hemp Channel,
> Seattle, WA), Vivian McPeak, host, 1999

Bill Bradley

I like Bradley. . . like McCain, he can do that kind of straight-talk
thing. But he doesn't know how to be as aggressive a player in the
political world as he was in the basketball world. And he would
get taken out like Jimmy Carter, if he was to get in.

> —Television interview, THC (The Hemp Channel,
> Seattle, WA), Vivian McPeak, host, 1999

Jimmy Carter

Jimmy Carter is an honest man. He was an excellent dude, man. But he was so naive, and they just took him right out. He didn't really have a chance. People say that they want a moral President. Well, they had one but they didn't give him a second term.

—Television interview, THC (The Hemp Channel, Seattle, WA), Vivian McPeak, host, 1999

Colin Powell

I'm so frustrated [with the current political system] that I also am being somewhat seduced by Colin Powell. The thing is, the Army is a collective. The Army is not like civilian life. An Army doctor gets paid his salary, but he doesn't get paid extra money for doing fancy stuff. He just gets paid his salary. You know, an Army doctor is probably at least a colonel and probably makes a good living. But he is not paid piecework like a civilian doctor, and he's not going to become a millionaire on being a doctor. An Army doctor is basically a public health doctor. And everybody who is in administration in the Army, a little piece of them is public health. Because they're running a big thing, and they're running it economically, and everybody must get covered. Because somebody is a private does not mean they get worse housing or worse medical care or worse clothing or crappier weapons than somebody of a higher rank. When it's not out killing people [the Army is] altruistic and it takes care of all the troops—officers and men and their wives and their dependents and their birthings. And do you know what? Army hospitals have fewer C-sections than private hospitals. Because it's not in anybody's interest for there to be any more, the way it is in private hospitals. Nobody makes any more money on it.

A guy who runs something like that is different from some-body who's run a business.

Another thing people worry about is, is [Powell] gonna have trouble being a black man in a "white" scene? The thing is, for the last how many years, any time he's entered a room, many white men have popped to attention, and stood at attention until he put them at ease! Which goes a lot toward taking off your black paranoia.

He claims to be part Jewish. He claims to be part Scots. He claims to be part Arowak Indian, you know, claims to be part Irish. Multi-cultural candidate—all of the stuff. His folks are from Jamaica. And he goes down to Jamaica and all the old rag-head grannies come out and hug him and love him. It's a dynamite show, I don't see how it can miss. I also understand exactly what his wife is afraid of. This is a racist country.

—Unpublished interview with Paul English, William Meyers,
Stephany Evans, and Marc Greene, 1995

Ralph Nader

They say, "What can you do better than Nader can do?"
And I say, "Register hippies."

—Television interview, THC (The Hemp Channel,
Seattle, WA), Vivian McPeak, host, 1999

Bill Clinton

I'd been asked what I thought about Bill on videotape, before the election, so I have it on record. I said I thought he was a "weenie." And they said, "What do you mean by a 'weenie'?" I said, "You know what a weenie is. He's a weenie."

And he is. My god, he's the biggest weenie in the free world. And we get ruled by his weenie.

The main thing I care about that stuff is that he lost so much credibility that he couldn't do anything about [drug czar] Mc-Caffery and he couldn't do anything about a lot of stuff, because he didn't have enough slack left over to complain about anything. He was hanging on by his eyelids. We had to put up with McCaffery.

If he was grounded in a mandate and had a good reputation, he'd say, "No! We're not gonna put the United States under mar-

tial law, because somebody wants us to have a dope czar! Where
the hell is a czar in the Constitution anyway?"

—Television interview, THC (The Hemp Channel,
Seattle, WA), Vivian McPeak, host, 1999

Libertarians

If you want to see a Libertarian get tongue-tied, ask him about his
health care system. It comes down to "Don't get sick."

• • •

Sometimes I think Libertarians are just Republicans who smoke
dope.

• • •

Libertarians are people who don't know that it is the government
who connects their driveways so they can go see each other.

Gays and Hippies

The other presidential seekers don't mention hippies and gay people. They've written off 20 percent of the population and ignored
massive injustice.

My Campaign

The thing that made me decide to run for President was that I
found myself approaching the age of 65, the age when folks
think of retiring. And I looked around. . . and my country has
become less free every year since I first noticed what the country was like. And it's been losing the ideals that it lived by. And
I've been studying that for years. And I'm not alone. There's a

lot of other really good people studying this thing of how we're losing it.

And I just came to the point where I felt that the war on drugs was one of the symptoms of the general unresponsiveness of the government, and evidence of its general bought-and-sold nature... and that we have had enough scientific evidence to turn this war on marijuana over for decades. Everybody knows that. I mean, everybody who's been following this... I know you guys all read the books I read... the study they did in India in the 1850s, where they said it wasn't a big deal, and the La Guardia study said it wasn't a big deal... and they got up to the Nixon study and the World Health Organization study, and they all say the same thing: No big deal, and like that. And that clear evidence is ignored, in the same way that Proposition 215 was ignored in California: If a people's referendum is not the hot, beating heart of democracy, I don't know what is.

And I thought: I gotta fight this.

And I feel like I've been training all my life for something like this, because I've been out doing politics when I was always being asked on camera... who I slept with and what I smoked... so many times that I've begun getting totally amused by it.

So I thought, I'll run for President, and I'll try to make enough noise to put the issues on the table.

• • •

However lowly you may think my status is in this race, you have to admit that I outlasted Orrin Hatch, Steve Forbes, Gary Bauer, Lamar Alexander, Lyndon LaRouche, Bill Bradley, John McCain, Alan Keyes, and Elizabeth Dole.

I got phone calls from Lyndon LaRouche guys trying to lean on me, and I said, "Well actually I've got to admit that I've thought LaRouche was nuts for years."

—Television interview, THC (The Hemp Channel,
Seattle, WA), Vivian McPeak, host, 1999

Stephen at a Green Party rally.

PART II

A Reader

CHAPTER 9

Being a Hippy

Hippies were revolutionaries, and as Che Guevara said, "A revolutionary is moved by great feelings of love."

I saw the hippies and fell in love with them because they were so fresh, and so new, and so clean in their intention and ideals. And I took their ideas, meditated on them, pondered them, cleaned them up, edited them, and have given them back.

Then when they got into my stuff, they'd often say, "This is what I was thinking myself."

I'd laugh and say, "Yeah. . . that's where I got it."

• • •

Being in the Marine Corps caused me to be set back a generation. When I went to school on the G.I. Bill, I [entered] with that year's crop of high schoolers when I'd just done time in Korea. I started hearing about beatniks.

I went to the Café Frankenstein in Laguna Beach [California], where they had the tombstone from the Frankenstein movies and black turtleneck sweaters and espresso and all that. I admired that and I went back and started one of those in San Bernardino, and I was a beatnik. [Beatniks were an intellectual movement.] I had a coffeehouse because beatniks were running on coffee and wine. When the hippies happened, I was socked into being a beatnik, because beatniks were veterans. Beatniks wore Army field jackets—that was usually the only warm coat they had. And beatniks had this kind of blunt, longish hair and longish beard, but not real long—just sort of this blunt cut thing [growing] out from all over at once. I was a beatnik, and I dug Kerouac and Dylan Thomas—not Gary Snyder, I didn't get into him until later. And not Ginsberg—I'm almost the same age as those guys, so I was working on the previous generation who were all drinkers. And then I started tracking with the hippies, and I started turning on, which kind of made sense—it went together and all.

What happened, my students came to me and said, "You've got to go see [the Beatles film] *A Hard Day's Night.*" They said, "You're popular, and we like you, but you have to go see that because you don't know what's going on." And then Timothy Leary started dropping acid on everyone. There was a young student [who] came to me and said, "I'm looking for a hippy boyfriend." I said, "I know this guy who's a poet." And this guy used to read his poetry, like in clubs in North Beach. And she went out with him and she came back and said, "That is *not a hippy!*"

Beatniks were more hung up in machismo than hippies. Hippies grew their hair long and didn't care if they were pretty, and a lot of them were like teenage boys and they were gorgeous. And then the hippy girls said, "We're not going to lay those short-hair Army boys. We're going to lay those pretty long-hair boys who don't go to war." And then all the boys wanted to grow their hair out, when they found out that was how you got laid. It was a cultural *Lysistrata* and it was really rewarded: Make Love, Not War. That stuff was really strong.

—Unpublished interview with Paul English, William Meyers,
Stephany Evans, and Marc Greene, 1995

• • •

We, the hippies, the same ones who people said were "dropping out," were the same ones who when someone said that Haight Street was dirty, brought down a pick-up full of brooms and swept it. And built People's Park in Berkeley. And everyone got into it. And that's because it wasn't just "Don't Bogart that joint." It was also "Don't Bogart that housing," "Don't Bogart that food," and "Don't Bogart that opportunity." That simple thing of "Don't Bogart it" gets into a whole lifestyle.

• • •

The hippy values are not just about talking about things and making motions about things but about doing things, putting your time into things. Being a hippy means being a doer.

One of the [ways] we on the Farm* learned to be doers was from the hippy skills for throwing a big party—something where you needed to set up multi-thousand-dollar sound systems, security systems, and lights. Our first technical crew, on the Farm, were the "roadies." They set up a ham radio for us.

• • •

When I hear people talk about hippies dropping out, I think about how I've climbed the fence into nuclear power plants; I've gone to Washington, DC, and directly lobbied and challenged for issues.

• • •

During Jimmy Carter's term, we saw these guys called "Sweat Equity" on a Bill Moyers special. They were rehabbing burned-out buildings. And we said, "Those guys are just like us." So we went to the Bronx to see all these black cats with big naturals with hard hats perched on top of them. So we came in, and they thought we were just like them. And they said, "OK, we'll teach you guys how to rehab buildings and how to get the city to give you papers on the buildings once you've got them rehabbed." And we showed them about vegetarian diets, about delivering babies, and about beginning an ambulance service—things that we on the Farm had learned for ourselves in order to take care of ourselves [and] to be

---

* Founded in 1971 in Summertown, Tennessee, the Farm became the fastest-growing counterculture community in the United States, with 1300 residents by 1977.

as independent as we wanted to be. Learning these things for ourselves, figuring out these problems for ourselves, made it so that
we could help other people.

So we went into the South Bronx with Plenty, the Farm's relief
organization, and started an ambulance service.

At the time, the cops had a bumper sticker that said, "Next
time you want help, call a Hippy." So we made a bumper sticker
that said, "Next time you want help, call a Hippy. Plenty Ambulance Service." We took the sarcastic phrase the cops were using
and redeemed it.

And that wasn't just a little bit of bravado on our part, because
our ambulance service won the Jefferson Award in the South
Bronx. In fact the New York Medical Service would go back and
complain to the city, "Well, the hippies got there first, again."

Then this bank liked us and gave us a bunch of money, and
they came into the city and said, "Look, it's not 'The hippies got
there first again' — their ambulance is newer."

Our ambulance service went everywhere. We could go into
tenements and shooting galleries and bring out people who had
OD'd, and we could clean up after gang fights. And the gangs
would give us honor guards. They would take care of us and es-
cort us into places that were dangerous. And they'd say, "Nobody
mess with Plenty."

I rode in New York City with the Plenty Ambulance Service.
Going down the streets, man, the toughest-looking guys would
look up at us and say, "Hey, Plenty! Hey, man!" We won their respect—as long-hairs, as hippies.

We took care of the South Bronx until the City of New York
realized that they were dogging it—and came back and put services back in the Bronx again.

Then after we'd gotten established in the South Bronx, the Indians in Akwesasne—in upstate New York—had an election, and
for the first time Uncle Julius and the Indians won. They then sent
home the cops from the nearby white town, saying, "We'd rather
have our own cops." But the local ambulance service then told
them, "We don't feel safe without cops, and we can't be here"—so
they split. So we came in with our ambulances we'd bought, had
guys who were paramedic trainers, went to one of the big phar-

maceutical companies and got training materials and a resuscitation doll and medical equipment. Then we set up an ambulance service that became the Indians' own ambulance service. They just moved right into the old police headquarters, hooked up their radios to the police's old antennas—and it became their territory.

Then in February of 1976, we went to Guatemala, immediately after the earthquake. We saw not only the earthquake damage, but also the obvious signs of poverty and starvation on every level, which caused us immediately to try to start a project in Guatemala.

First we took carpenters, and we rebuilt after the earthquake. Then we took medical personnel and tried to open and help with clinics. We didn't receive a lot of cooperation from the government for our medical operations, but we found that we could do diet and nutrition with their blessing. Our path was always to stay clear and not cause trouble that could draw down fire on the local residents, who live completely at the mercy of the government.

Our project prospered in Guatemala, and we learned not only Spanish, but Indian dialects: Cakchiquel, Quiche. Our work and friendship with the Guatemalan people seemed to be completely open-ended. It looked as if we could stay there and initiate projects and raise money in the United States and really get to be of help for a lot of people who came to be our close friends. But as the situation in Nicaragua turned over, as the situation in El Salvador smoldered into a civil war, the character of Guatemala became changed as the velvet lining on the iron glove began to wear through.

University professors were killed. Students were killed. Civilian political candidates were killed, sometimes shot down in the street, sometimes hunted down by motorized death squads driving cars with government plates carrying men in civilian clothes with military weapons.

Then the focus shifted from the city to the country. Whole villages were massacred. They systematically shot the people who were working on literacy programs, radio communications programs, people's medical programs, and agricultural extension help programs, because those people were organizers, and the organizers must be removed right off the top. Plenty was forced to pull its volunteers home. Sadly, we embraced those friends we left behind and brought as many as we could with us. We returned to the United States.

We hated to leave. We didn't leave from fear. We left because our presence was a temptation that could bring down fire on the Indians.

• • •

I was already at a point where somebody might consider that I was a grownup: I was teaching in college, a veteran, married with kids. . . all that kind of stuff. And these young people came up— and the thing that they did that so fascinated me was they looked at the world in a fresh way and thought how it should be. . . and wanted to know why it wasn't that way.

And that was so simple.

I knew that there was something in the mystical turnover of the generations about that, because the youth are the ones who see how far the grownups have fallen short of their ideals. And we need that to happen to every generation.

That's redeeming.

Deeming something is to make an estimate about it, like in the phrase "I deem it just." So redeeming is to look at something and say, "What is this?" and "What do we really want it to be about?" To re-estimate it.

I saw in the questions the kids were asking in the '60s that we'd come far from the idealism that's expressed in the Constitution.

• • •

I wasn't political in those days, and it was mainly because, though I realized where it was at, I thought if I tried to live these ideals, I would find myself on a collision course with the establishment.

• • •

What hippies taught us through their protests, massive music concerts, and sit-ins is that we can do big things together.

• • •

We have to do demonstrations again and show power that doesn't belong to the corporation, doesn't belong to the church, doesn't belong to the state, but belongs to the people. I love the youth of the Seattle WTO protests and the DC a16 action.

• • •

The youth of the '60s took on the civil rights movement, took on the anti-war movement. They took on Nixon and the excesses of government. They came out for everything that they thought was wrong, and if they could identify it, they got up a movement for it.

• • •

I don't talk about "plastic hippies," the posers, or the ones who were spacey, damaged from too much drugs and all that kind of stuff. They were not really the majority. Because of them, though, the people out in the middle of the United States often couldn't tell the Hell's Angels from the Hari Krishnas.

We could, though.

The vast majority of hippies were folks who had school, and families, and homes, and jobs, and could only afford to do it part time. But they still had that ideal.

Like when I was in college, one of my girlfriends was the one who raised the Panamanian flag on campus. Another one of my girlfriends went to Selma, Alabama, with a station wagon full of books and started a library.

I saw my job as being to show the hippies what their potential was and inspire them to do all the good work they could do helping out the country.

• • •

I consider hippies to be anyone from radical lesbians to Hell's Angels.

• • •

I had a meeting with 1500 people at my Monday night class [a weekly meeting where politics, religion, acid, sex, and love were discussed openly] and it was immediately after the students had been shot at Kent State. There were a bunch of hard-core political guys who said we should get some guns together.

And I was fighting that.

While I was fighting that, somebody gave me a piece of candy which, I didn't know at the time, had about 500 micrograms of acid on it. But soon I realized what they'd given me, and at a point I asked if I could go outside and come on. They said, "No, you've gotta finish the argument."

So I'm coming on very heavy. And I had to sit there and come on to all of that, and carry on this discussion about whether we should go get guns or not.

It got to the point where I realized that the guys who were talking violence were a little fringe of about 75 or 80 people around the back of the crowd.

And I said, "You know I've been comin' here for weeks and weeks with you guys, and I've been talkin' peace and love and you guys've been saying 'Yeah, yeah,' you know. And I've been talkin' peace and love, and you guys say, 'Yeah, yeah.' And I've been talkin' peace and love. . . ."

And the audience said, "Yeah. . . yeah": It was the other 1400 people, who were not into getting guns, making themselves heard.

And when they said that, I said, "Thank you for that. . . and can I go out and come on now?"

And they said, "Yes, you can."

• • •

It's easy to talk about the hippy movement as if it was an aggregate, but it wasn't an aggregate. It was a whole bunch of kids from a whole bunch of states.

The bands held us together because that was something we could do in great big ventures together and derive a little culture.

• • •

There was a television special called "The Pig in the Python." It's a lovely bit of television about the Baby Boomers. In the program the narrator pointed out that before the hippies, nobody'd ever thought of teenagers as a separate group of people. . . and then, when they got to be hippies, they became a separate country.

• • •

The hippies were never supposed to take over the world. What we are is a continuing strain of artists, writers, musicians, activists, socially conscious folks, and folks who are on the fringe who see ways that society could be doing better and are trying to do something about it.

Society can get really complacent if no one takes care of that part for them. . . and that's our, the hippies', job.

In Europe such people are kind of enshrined and respected, much more so than here.

But we're not supposed to take over the world. Instead, we're like a vitamin or trace element, in that no society is healthy without us.

• • •

There's the legislative, the executive, and the judicial branch—and then we call the press "the Fourth Estate."

The Fifth Estate, to me, is the several million hippies in the street. They're as much a part of the government as anybody.

• • •

In the Caravan,* we didn't take welfare.

I was teaching that the idea of a begging monk was out of date, because the world was too poor for anyone to beg. There

---

* Known as the Caravan, this refers to a 1970 speaking tour of the United States involving more than 300 participants in 60 school buses and about 40 campers.

could be no class of people who begged as a discipline because they didn't have any other way to make it. A monk has to earn his keep.

I was of the idea that it shouldn't be that if you were religious, you had the right to be some kind of drag on society.

So I thought that working to make it was one of the things we were supposed to do. . . that we were a mutant strain of hippies who were not bummed by work. Folks who can take care of themselves, should.

We were not a bunch of people who had any ailments or such. We were a bunch of people who were in quite good condition—physically and mentally—and we were going to build a new life. The last thing in the world we wanted to do was to have anybody in the government be able to tell us anything or have anything to do with us whatsoever.

It's nice to have the government taking care of you, but if the government takes care of you, they are justified in having some information about you. They get to know whether you are on welfare with a meth lab in the basement!

• • •

I consider myself to be an ethnic hippy. By that I mean that the ethnicity I grew up with was such a white-bread, skim-milk, gringo experience that it wasn't satisfying for me. It had no moxie. Now, being a hippy, that's another thing. I feel like the Sioux feel being from the Lakota Nation. I feel like Mario Cuomo feels about being Italian. It makes me feel close with Jews and Rastafarians. I have a tribe, too.

—"Monday Night Class, The New Edition" (unpublished)

• • •

Hippies are the largest untapped pool of voters. I think that there's enough of them to make the difference, if they would only do it.

And that's who I am, and that's who I'm talking to.

And I think that there's some squares who're going to like me. Some of the same kind of people who like McCain are going to like me. . . quite a few of them.

—Television interview, THC (The Hemp Channel, Seattle, WA), Vivian McPeak, host, 1999

• • •

I joined the Marine Corps in 1952, got out in '55. I think I would be described these days as having post-traumatic stress syndrome: It took me six years to get to AA.

A lot of beer was involved in that, too.

Then I discovered, here I am, I've got a new baby, and I need to straighten up. I went to San Francisco, and I cut my hair, and I got a sport coat, and sat in front-row center, and took the instructors to coffee and answered all the questions and did my homework. I got on the Dean's List. . . and graduated cum laude.

I mean, it was a certain amount of hassle to get mad at 'em and walk out on 15 units of withdraw "F," and then have to come back and beg my way back in as a veteran.

So, eventually, I taught at San Francisco State College, and that was fun. The thing I saw was these young people who had no permission from any agency of church or state to do what they were doing. They were world-class and huge, and they got bigger and bigger.

And, they got me. I said, "Oh, I never considered the option that people like us had any power. That's an exciting option, man."

And I fell in love with the hippies just completely. My mother says, they got my mind. . . and she was right.

—Television interview, THC (The Hemp Channel, Seattle, WA), Vivian McPeak, host, 1999

CHAPTER 10

Campaign Finance and Political Office Reforms

I want to give us a fair chance at running our country. . . which starts with campaign finance.

Campaign finance reform is not going to get much better until people start calling some portions of it "bribery."

• • •

Our children need to know that what's being done is that our legislators are being bribed. . . and they're just passing laws to make it look better.

• • •

How do we make sure that the people in power use their power correctly? You have elections and campaign finance reform. You've got to be able to fire the guys who are screwing up. If you can't fire them, then you can't do anything anyway.

• • •

You can't have the kind of system that's locked up. The old emperors used to have 75-year reigns. Men could live and die under the same emperor. . . and never would it ever be malleable, so there'd be a chance for [something] else to happen.

I think it was wise to change the law after Roosevelt was elected for the fourth time. He had so many people he'd helped that they were going to vote for him for the rest of his life.

• • •

Two terms in office is plenty. . . and for some people, too many.

• • •

The way that the seniority and the chairmanship of the important [Congressional] committees and all that other important stuff works is just as screwed up as the other part. You've got to break up the good ol' boy network. You can't permit that sort of fossilization of the people's systems.

• • •

Politicians tell the public how they're going to work things out when they get into office. . . then they promise the public they'll give that solution to them. So they go into office with a set of instructions.

I mostly don't like the idea of getting a set of instructions about how to do something until I've tried to figure it out for myself.

What I want to talk about is that we get the crooks out of government and fix it so that the businesses can't buy the government. Then, when we've got the government so it's kind of functional, we can find out what it can do.

We don't even know what it can do right now, because as soon as [some people] realize it can make a difference to their profit margin, they start trying to take over the government and subvert the democratic process.

It is considered somehow OK to subvert the democratic process for the purpose of profit. It is not OK to do that.

• • •

Politicians are a craven lot. They can't tell the people anything true that the people would actually like, so they have to be creative in how they lie to them, since they're actually going to vote on behalf of the people who bought them.

That puts them in a little bit of a bind to have anything to talk about. What they're going to do is what the corporations want them to do. So they give you some jive.

Campaign finance reform is absolutely necessary to do anything about any of that, because you have to have honest legislators before anything can be done.

—Television interview, THC (The Hemp Channel, Seattle, WA), Vivian McPeak, host, 1999

Stephen mans the Green table in Athens, Georgia.

CHAPTER 11

Corporations

I don't believe in the death penalty for people, but I do believe in it for corporations.

A corporation is not a person.

Back just after Lincoln died, the Supreme Court—in the Santa Clara decision—[ruled] that a corporation was a person. . . had the rights and privileges of a person.

Then later on [about 1910] that was strengthened. In 1978, in the Griswold decision, they said that not only is a corporation a person but it has Constitutionally protected free speech, and its money is its free speech. Which is like sort of a one-man, one-vote idea: There's me, one man, and then there's General Motors. I get to have my vote and it gets to use its money. . . not even thinking about the fact that it has eternal life and can be many places at once.

And that's an evil thing.

—Television interview, THC (The Hemp Channel,
Seattle, WA), Vivian McPeak, host, 1999

• • •

Everything is priced so high and designed so that you can't make it if your household doesn't have two jobs. Ordinary peoples' buying power is now such—if you adjust for inflation—that they're making less money than they were in the 1960s. Meanwhile, people at the top of the big corporations—the golden parachute and buy-out guys—are making more money than has ever been made by anyone in the history of money.

We have the largest gap going between rich and poor that this country has ever seen. Other countries marvel at it.

I used to rank on the British about their class system. But it pales to what's going on here. What's going on here is class war. We're talking class war that's being carried on intentionally by people who at the same time swear that they believe in the Prince of Peace.

This class war has, in my lifetime, transformed this country into a caricature of what it was when I was a kid.

I cannot stand that.

• • •

Corporations are not the weather. You've got to be philosophical about how you meet the weather. It's what it is and you've got to put up with it.

But it's not an accident that the corporations are regarded as persons: Supreme Court justices were bought to bring that to happen. We don't have to stand for it. We can fix it if we all work together.

• • •

There are frailties that are common to humanity. But it is the job of intelligent and enlightened humanity to create structures that overcome them, rather than create structures that enhance them. But the direction of the corporations worldwide is to enhance human frailty for the bottom line. They don't always sell bad things. They'll sell you something that's good if it makes money.

• • •

There's this view about "the good Germans." It says that "the good Germans" were just as bad as the other ones because what went down went down on their watch and in their country, too—and though they, the "good Germans," didn't like it, they didn't do anything about it. But what's not said is that if these "good

Germans" tried to do something about their circumstances, it meant walking into the face of the Gestapo. It meant facing being shot down like a dog by people who had the power to shoot people down like dogs and nobody'd dare raise an eyebrow.

In our country, power is more insidiously maintained. People don't necessarily have to fear being shot down in the streets just because they have opposing points of view. If ordinary persons don't speak out about some injustice, then, it's popular to blame them for selling out to the system. But it's like the Don Marquis poem about the worm that was eaten by the robin and says, "This shows the ways that birds have always imposed on worms. The things that you do to me are so totally unfair. Why should I have to give up my whole life and viewpoint just so some bird can be fed?" So we take the worm's side and put a judgment on the bird.

But if you get a little farther down in the bird's intestinal tract, you begin to see the bird's point. You begin to think, "Well, a bird's got to eat."

And people have to eat.

But the system is rigged in such a way that in order to eat, people have to give up their will to speak out.

That's unfair.

It's a form of slavery—which is what corporations hope for. This is a kind of slavery in which the corporations don't have to own the slaves, they just rent them. If they can tie the people down with enough velvet chains to enough television sets so they can't walk away from them, and convince them that they are consumers, they've got them.

• • •

When you have the amount of money that the corporations have, the amount of science they can purchase, the computers and all the stuff they have behind them to implement their whims, then ordinary people aren't the problem and individually don't have a chance.

What you have to do about it is [see to it] that the corporations, which are machines, are ruled by people who breathe.

• • •

We were all told that last year we had a terrible flu season. But now the true story has broken: We had the average, ordinary, normal flu season that we always have. But two drug companies came out with competing flu medicines and did a media blitz. And that's why the whole world thought they had a bad flu season last year when they didn't.

The corporations huffed up a flu epidemic so they could sell their stuff.

And the media were complicit in it: Every news anchor went along with the story as if it was real.

• • •

There's wickedness afoot. But the thing about wickedness is that it's not about the devil having the master plan. It's about the fact that it's already hard enough to do right in the first place. If, then, you're a little off balance because you have a society that rewards people for being rich by allowing them to beat the law, it's even harder to keep trying to do what's right.

• • •

Somebody said that things get pretty confusing when we see Michael Jordan on the screen beside Bill Bradley, endorsing him, and then a few minutes later we see Michael Jordan on the screen beside Bugs Bunny. That remark might be why Michael quit doing endorsements.

• • •

After the Civil War, Lincoln said he was more afraid of the power that corporations gained during the war than the damage the war did to the country itself.

And Eisenhower said that the clearest danger to freedom and democracy in the world was the power of the military/industrial complex.

• • •

The problem is that we've been reading the guarantees on Proctor and Gamble and other such products, thinking that we were dealing with businesses that were being honest, while the businesses were going around buying the state legislatures piece by piece, buying the congressmen piece by piece, buying the senators, until they could buy everything they wanted. And there've been tremendous efforts to try and stop it.

When I was young, grown-ups used to cuss Roosevelt. I didn't understand why they were always cussing Roosevelt. Then as I got older, I realized what he had done: He had taken down the big corporations, man. . . he had busted the trusts. And he had given jobs to poor people.

He had done such things that it's amazing he wasn't assassinated for the things he did. Ronald Reagan wasn't the Anti-Christ; he was just the Anti-Roosevelt.

• • •

The problem in our modern times is that it's possible for corporations to buy up all the televisions and newspapers and not let there be any opposing opinions. Which in great measure has been done.

• • •

Today, when corporations do something that seems to be for the public benefit, it's for the corporation's public relations and they expect to get paid back for it. They're not doing it out of any altruistic reason whatsoever. They do that kind of stuff because it's good business.

• • •

We're living in the age of the bottom line, and the charters of the corporations are written in such a way that any guy that works for the corporation and doesn't pay attention to the bottom line, doesn't get to work for that corporation. The corporations are selectively winnowing out anybody with any morals or conscience whatsoever, because they're inconvenient when it comes to making profit.

• • •

On the average, the bigger the corporation gets, the more likely it is to be operating for greed.

• • •

How come Royal Dutch Shell had a pass in Vietnam and could drive across the Vietnamese and American lines. . . could drive right in and right out, and the Vietnamese didn't bomb their oil refineries while everybody else's were getting bombed? Don't you think Shell had some deal with somebody?

• • •

Corporations under proper control could be a boon to the world. They're not intrinsically bad. But they have been given powers, frequently by dishonest legislators who were bought for the purpose of giving them those powers, that they have no right to have, and they use those powers against society. The way the law about corporations was written is that a corporation should serve the public good. It used to be on the books in most venues that you could take a corporation's charter and make them sell their assets and take them out of business for not doing right. These days they're going around and taking that little law off the books everywhere they can find it—buying the local venues and [getting rid of] those laws.

• • •

It used to be that the Kansas City baseball team had some people from Kansas on it.

And it used to be that Americans owned American businesses.

• • •

When the corporations went multinational was one of the real breaking points. That's when the corporations had more in common with each other than with their home countries. Corporations today are no longer competing. Capitalism is supposed to be about competition. Well, the corporations aren't competing with anybody except the citizens.

• • •

Anyone in a corporation, except for the absolute top guys, is always expendable and interchangeable.

• • •

When I'm talking about corporations, I'm not blaming every guy with a red star on the front of his shirt who's pumping gas. I am not talking about them. When I talk about corporations, I'm talking about the guys who in collusion in these boardrooms on interlocking directorates—the guys who are on the boards of several companies at once—get together and fix prices internationally.

• • •

Talk about venal. When Wayne Andres at [Archer Daniels Midland] got caught doing international price fixing on one of the essential amino acids—lycene—he let his son take the fall and go to jail for him, rather than do it himself. And his son went to jail for that. And it was proven that ADM was doing it and they were in it with several other worldwide companies. . . fixing the price of an essential amino acid!

• • •

The tobacco industry was in deep shit a year or so ago. We really had them back against the wall. Then all of a sudden there's this $44 million industry advertising campaign pointing out that the same politicians who smoke cigars won't let you smoke cigarettes.

• • •

Our top priority is to change the laws that govern the corporations. If we don't change those laws, the corporations will eat us alive.

But there are people who do not want to change those laws for any reason other than it will enhance their ability to make more money.

And they're already making too much money.

• • •

John D. Rockefeller used to carry a pocket full of dimes, so when anybody came up to him and talked to him about money, he'd give 'em a dime and say, "I've had it figured out. . . that's your share."

• • •

The corporations of the '50s were pussycats compared to the ones we have now. The ones we have now are global—they're not responsible to any country, they don't want to be responsible to any country, and they don't want any government to tell them anything. The World Trade Organization, as it is set up and is intended to work, can override laws passed inside sovereign countries.

• • •

What scares and worries me today is the absolute, ironclad, totalitarian control of corporate fascism.

• • •

There's no such thing as a free-market economy. Corporations not only don't want to lose any money in a free market, they want to make you insure them if they do.

• • •

Corporations are machines. Never take any shit from a machine.

• • •

I don't want to be a damn consumer. I don't want to be considered to fit into the system in that way. The idea that people who have to buy the things to keep the corporations going are thought of as "consumers" shows how the corporations really think about them: they're nothing but an end place for the corporate products to land.

We need to have someone who makes the corporations do right. Not someone who says, "We'd like to have you not poison us as much, please." I'm not interested in that kind of relationship with corporations.

• • •

What the guys who run the corporations tell us is, "Well, we can't do anything about how things are; we're responsible to the stockholders to maximize our profit."

Well, they've got to rewrite the way that works then. That's a trash producer, a people killer, and a freedom taker.

• • •

Resistance against the corporations is going to be hard. We're going to have to be brave about it.

At the same time that my girlfriend in college was cataloging the library thing in Selma, I was in Washington, DC, with the Mississippi Challenge, trying to not seat the Mississippi delegate—because Bobby Kennedy had said that they didn't have voter rights in Mississippi. And I got to hang out with Stokley Carmichael and other civil rights workers. And I listened to them talking to one another and asking, "What happened to ol' so-and-so?"

"Oh, he got hit in the head so many times he quit making sense."

That was them talking about their being beaten in the streets and their heroes and casualties.

And they were very brave. White kids were inspired by that.

And Martin Luther King inspired white people as well as black people at that time.

When Martin Luther King started talking economic justice and getting out of Vietnam, he didn't last much longer: There's a little bit of sympathy for racial justice, but not as much for economic justice.

That's why this is not just a race problem but a class war.

• • •

With the way the corporations have run [things] with the collaboration of the Supreme Court, with the bought Court decisions and stuff like that, the people's rights are so badly eroded at this point there's hardly anything you can do about it.

The only thing you *can* do about it—short of taking up arms— is to register every hippy, every dope smoker, every health fooder, every home schooler. . . just right down the line. Everybody on that whole side of the world has got to get registered.

And I am currently asking them to register Green, because I want there to be a huge, big, noticeable bump. If everybody registers Democrat or Republican, they'll just slide into the existing system and not be seen. But registering Green, there'll be a big tracer that shows that a lot of people are registering, and they're registering Green, and they might not vote for you guys.

And that would scare 'em some.

We need to scare 'em some.

—Television interview, THC (The Hemp Channel,
Seattle, WA), Vivian McPeak, host, 1999

• • •

The guys who are really raping the planet—the golden-parachute guys and the like—are not stupid. They know what they're doing. They're just getting theirs now while the getting's good. That's why there should be sanctions on the corporate predators.

That's why I say that I'm not for the death penalty for people but for corporations. We should give corporations a few warnings, and if they don't radically change and have some part of their energy devoted to the public interest, take them out. Make them sell their assets and start over.

• • •

The big corporations have to play by the same ground rules that other people do.

• • •

We, as a government, endow universities and research outfits to do pure research, out of which pharmaceutical companies take drugs they make money on. And they charge high prices for those drugs, because they say that research costs a lot of money, when they were subsidized by the government.

That's corporate welfare.

• • •

We have to make it so that you can't accept a contribution from business interests. I mean at city, state, and federal levels that you should not be allowed to have businesses donate money to candidates. Those donations should only come from private individuals.

And then what you do is you only allow so big an expenditure for a particular level of office. We already see that people are spending more money to get into office than that office would make them in 50 years.

Campaign finance reform. . . to bring that about is a major revolution. That revolution starts with people. I got a letter from Pete Seeger, saying, "Have you guys thought of the Farm as being like Highlander Institute,* and trying to train some activists?" Stuff like that.

—Unpublished interview for *Free Spirit* magazine, with Paul English, William Meyers, Stephany Evans, and Marc Greene, 1995

• • •

---

*Highlander Institute is Miles Horton's place down in Tennessee. You may not have heard of it as the Highlander Institute, but they are the outfit that trained Rosa Parks. Martin Luther King used to go hang out there. Rosa Parks went directly from a Miles Horton Highlander meeting to the front of that bus.

There's also a guy named Paul Hawken, who was a businessman for a while and then said that we can't look at the business balance sheets to make our business decisions. We have to look at the balance sheets of the world, at what's happening with the environment, and go into the real balance sheets about our business—the other ones are fake. He came to this realization after working in business for a while—he took freshman English from me back at San Francisco State College. The thing that he's about right now—the change that he has made—may have been easier for him because he came from being a hippy. But that's the kind of change that a lot of business guys have got to do. Paul Hawken's and Amory Lovins' and L. Hunter Lovins' new book, *Natural Capitalism*, will be a help for those guys. I give him an "A" for the book.

The idea that the bottom line is the most important thing in business is definitely the philosophy right now. AT&T, after having built itself into this huge conglomerate, is now breaking itself up into three chunks, and the process of breaking itself up into those three chunks is now canceling out another 8,400 jobs. And every time it merged, it canceled out jobs, too. And now in its unmerging it's still canceling out jobs and we have the phenomenon of "business is good," while the people who are all being laid off from those jobs suffer. I have people write me who want to be part of, and come live at, my Rocinante project. I got one letter from a guy out in California who went from being a university professor to being homeless in about six months.

—Unpublished interview for *Free Spirit* magazine, with Paul English, William Meyers, Stephany Evans, and Marc Greene, 1995

• • •

The real problem, the big problem, is the corporate-globalization, fascistic takeover of the world. That's the one that something's got to be done about. And I don't think that anybody but the United States of America has the financial muscle to oppose the corporations at any level.

If this country had the stuff to do what Roosevelt did—back [with] the old robber barons: the Rockefellers, and Carnegies, and Vanderbilts and all those guys. Man, he had his trust busters out.

And the trusts were like these mergers. . . these big guys getting together in clumps and getting stronger and stronger.

And Roosevelt busted that stuff.

That's one of the things that I admire most of any President in my lifetime. (The other one was Harry Truman firing Douglas MacArthur.)

—Television interview, THC (The Hemp Channel,
Seattle, WA), Vivian McPeak, host, 1999

• • •

I'm not as fearful of my government as I am of the corporate power structure, because the corporate power structure right now has the government on the ropes. And the only thing that can [fix] it is if you had enough guys who weren't bought, who could pass laws and say, "Companies that go off-shore to avoid taxes will have tariffs at the border to square it up if they want to do business in this country."

Screw that whole thing.

Nuts to the idea that corporations don't have to be responsible to anybody in the world. That's the main thing they're working at right now: to not be responsible to any country.

If the United States took the lead, there's a possibility that Australia and Canada and a few places like that might come along, and we'd be able to mount enough countries that could make enough laws to make a difference so that companies, if they want to do business in those countries, would have to be responsible for their actions in the first place.

And in the second place, as far as corporate taxes go, they should pay hefty taxes for the privilege of being able to do business in our country. They are made open to a population that's got a pretty good amount of money and is worth a lot. They should give excellent service and good guarantees and everything like that—right across the board, just automatically—and there should be no crap about any of that.

And the only way that can happen is if this country, which has enough rich people and enough buying power and enough world clout, tries hard to push the balance enough to make a difference. If they had to confine their business to every country but the U.S.A., it would cost them plenty.

—Television interview, THC (The Hemp Channel, Seattle, WA), Vivian McPeak, host, 1999

• • •

Capitalism means technically that the money rules. Not as a metaphor. That's just what capitalism is. . . that the decisions will be made for the sake of the money. That's what it is. That's what they call "the bottom line."

We've got to say, "If you produce a product, your cost-accounting for that product has got to include every damage to the environment made to manufacture it, and every amount of money that it takes to recycle it to not damage the ecology further when you take it out of service."

In Europe, Mercedes has got systems so they don't hook dissimilar stuff together in ways it's hard to get apart. . . so you don't have to have your plastic so riveted to your steel that it's a hassle to separate 'em to recycle them. They got stuff so it can come apart into types of component material.

Corporations need to take that burden on themselves. They need to not make the taxpayers pay for that. They need to take that on themselves. And there has to be a real idea of what the cost of stuff is. . . because if you're making something out of something irreplaceable, the cost ought to reflect it.

—Television interview, THC (The Hemp Channel, Seattle, WA), Vivian McPeak, host, 1999

• • •

A corporation is basically a machine. And if the corporations rule, we're being ruled by robots.

If you want to get metaphysical about it, the definition of a demon is something that has ambition and power and has drives for growth and defense of itself, but it doesn't have a soul. It does have powers and can do things, which is really a pretty good operating definition of a corporation.

That's got to be harnessed. And the only thing that can harness that is a fair process and an informed electorate. There's no other power in the world that can face it.

An informed electorate wouldn't have any problem with saying, "You come and pollute in our country. . . you not only clean up, but if we want to, we'll put up a way to keep you out."

Stephen and NYC cops, Million Marijuana March, 1998.

CHAPTER 12

Universal Health Care and Education

Lots of people are into the idea that everyone's got to have health care. But what most politicians are into is that the government should pay the insurance companies retail for it.

I'm saying let's kick the insurance companies out of things where it's inappropriate for them to be. The insurance companies are a lot like the Mafia—except for the concept of honor.

If you take the insurance companies out of the medical business, you don't have to buy those high-rise office buildings and pay for those golden parachutes and all that stuff, and you save enough money on that to insure the 47 million people who are not now insured.

• • •

Right now we have socialized medicine in this country, but the only people who get it are the military, and congressmen, and senators, and Cabinet officials, and Presidents, and Vice-Presidents and people like that.

The elderly have Medicare, but they don't get the quality of care that the military and Congress get. The military and Congress go to the same kinds of places that the President goes.

The elderly don't.

• • •

ır legislators is the guy who collected
are industry for proposing an alterna-
ınton's—that is, to take Clinton's out.
ırt surgeon and has $13 million of stock
of America], and his father founded
ve don't have two senators from Ten-
·s is from the Hospital Corporation of
ıder Tennessee's credentials.

w for *Free Spirit* magazine, with Paul English,
·yers, Stephany Evans, and Marc Greene, 1995

We're the only country among the industrialized, so-called civilized countries of the world that doesn't have socialized medicine.
Well, of course, it should be single-payer, it should come from the
government. We're the country where Hospital Corporation of
America is going around to other countries and buying hospitals
that are not for profit and taking them into profit. We're trying to
stop the rest of the world from having health care. But in actuality,
the rest of the world takes care of all of its citizens.

When I was up in Canada one time, I was talking about doctors, and this guy said, "Boy, you talk about your doctors bad.
How come you talk about your doctors so bad?"

I said, "Don't you talk about your doctors like that?"

He said, "No, our doctors take care of us."

Then someone else said, "Yeah. . . everybody has health care
here."

It blew my mind, 'cause I had been habitually pissed at doctors for a long time, and these guys did not feel like that.

That was some years ago. They might feel differently now,
though, since the Americans have been hammering away on their
system as hard as they can, 'cause it makes the Americans look so
rotten to have them next door, doing it so well and everybody
liking it.

• • •

That idea that there's something wrong with socialized medicine. . .
that's some kind of old anti-Commie bugaboo.

I ain't no Commie.

"Socialized" means that it's done for the sake of society.

• • •

Since we give these corporations absolute hunting and fishing
rights on the population to rip us off in every way they can devise,
shouldn't we at least be allowed to be healthy while we're being
ripped off?

• • •

I'm not advocating socialized medicine just for the poor but for everyone. Everyone gets the same kind, the same quality, of medical care that the congressmen and the President now get.

• • •

Whenever I look at something, I look at it with a public health attitude. . . and that goes for everything from some kinds of drugs being legalized and others not.

• • •

What we want is not-for-profit national health care.

• • •

We all pay for public health care, and we get it cheaper than letting the doctors run it on their own, without the government being in on it—because they would be profiteers.

It'll cost us less than what we're paying now. It would come out of taxes, and it would be in the government's interest to keep it economical.

That's the lesson to be learned from looking at all the other countries. All the other countries that have national health care are covered better than we are and spend less money from taxes for doing it.

• • •

I don't say that capitalism guarantees that everybody gets to be a millionaire. Guaranteeing that somebody gets to be a millionaire is a hell of a lot more wasteful and stupid than guaranteeing that everybody gets health.

• • •

Having public health care is not public assistance. It's just how we all take care of ourselves.

In Tennessee. . . one of
$600,000 from the health
tive health care plan to
One of our senators is a h
in [Hospital Corporation
HCA, you know, and so
nessee. One of our senat
America, and just works u

—Unpublished interv
William M

CHAPTER 13

Cannabis

I am not going to try to sell marijuana in this chapter with any cute and lyrical dope stories. I have done that in other places. I asked my revolutionary friend Steve Kubby for a little strategic advice about how to run this campaign. He told me two important things. The first was not to toke up for the cameras. It trivializes the whole thing. The other thing was not to try and sell pot. It needs no advertising. Make them justify the policies.

• • •

The war on drugs should just completely stop.

There are problems with addiction and heroin. That's why I've mostly spoken up for cannabis.

I personally liked LSD—and it didn't hurt me. But I know there's a small percentage of people (maybe one and a half or two percent) who get knocked so far off balance that they may never get back. And you can't advocate anything that has even a small percentage of something like that.

I don't feel bad saying that about grass. I think that grass is an awesomely benign substance—for the nice amount of relaxation, and insight, and empathy, and all the good stuff that's in it.

—Television interview, THC (The Hemp Channel, Seattle, WA), Vivian McPeak, host, 1999

• • •

I don't just say legalize cannabis, because I don't want to see the big tobacco companies step in and take over and advertise and make money off of our sacrament. Cannabis needs no advertising.

I don't think the growing and selling or trading of pot in moderate amounts among friends should be regulated at all. During alcohol prohibition, there was an allowance for people who had wine as a part of their culture and diet. It was called a "head of the household allowance." It was 600 gallons.

For large amounts I think of a state system like Oregon's state liquor stores. A plain building without advertising and government-regulated low retail prices for medical or recreational pot.

All pot prisoners who were not involved with guns, violence, or hard drugs should have amnesty and immediate release and purging of their criminal records.

I actually think that decriminalizing cocaine would confound the coke lords more than anything else, but that is not this fight. Decriminalizing cannabis should be allowed to run for a few years without complicating it, to learn how to do it. If it works, possibly an expansion could be considered.

I wouldn't mind a moderate tax in the state stores if it could be dedicated to education or helping fund Medicare or something worthwhile. But there should be absolutely no taxation at the personal or medical level.

—*Paradigm Shift* magazine interview by Philip H. Farber, 1998

• • •

I don't think children should use cannabis. When children get an early introduction to cannabis, too often they go immediately to the limits of habitation and supply. It becomes something that structures their time, and they neglect their education. If I had known I was going to need to remember my Spanish verbs for the rest of my life, I would have studied harder at the time. It's a lot harder to learn them now. I feel really strongly about children getting a good education. And that doesn't mean they all have to be businessmen or machinists. They all have different talents and their education should be flexible enough so that they get to develop those talents.

Back in the '60s, when we were freaking our brains out, a lot of people turned on kids who were too young. At the Farm, as we've evolved as a community, it has become evident that we'd rather our kids didn't start turning on early. We don't want to distract them from their essential kidness.

Keeping cannabis out of the hands of small children is one of the most important and difficult questions that hip parents as well as square parents face. You can't just depend on keeping it out of their hands, either. The best thing would be if you had never lied to them and you were friends and they would respect your wishes. A lot of our ethic came from young people and it is a mistake to think that they can't understand anything heavy.

—*Cannabis Spirituality*, pp. 94-95

• • •

I saw a woman on television, it's a sad thing, whose son had died from huffing something he'd gotten from under the kitchen sink. And she said, "God, I wish he'd been smoking pot."

—Television interview, THC (The Hemp Channel, Seattle, WA), Vivian McPeak, host, 1999

• • •

I think that we would save so much money by calling off the war on drugs that we could probably give tax write-offs and benefits to folks who have been locked up to make them not have to carry any tax burden while they got themselves together. I don't think that's an out-of-hand thing to do—because I know people who've been locked up.

I did a year in the Tennessee State Penitentiary myself. My lawyer got my voting rights back, and he was very good about it.

The Tennessee legislature made an ex post facto law—a retroactive law. You can't make something illegal retroactively: the law has got to start now, and then everything from now is going to be caught. . . . They [had] accidentally made a law that made it so that convicts were voting inside the pen. Then they tried to fix that. So when they tried to fix that, they made it retroactive to cover years that it'd been running. And my lawyer beat that, and it was a class action suit, and it got back voting rights for me—and in the 18 years since, it's probably got back voting rights for another quarter-million prisoners.

—Television interview, THC (The Hemp Channel, Seattle, WA), Vivian McPeak, host, 1999

Stephen and Rita Mauley, Amsterdam, 1977, at the Cannabis Cup. This international cannabis competition is held every year.

CHAPTER 14

Women

There has been holocaust on women several times in history.

I'm worse in my ire about how women have been treated than I am in my ire about corporations.

• • •

The Church claims there's an intrinsic evilness in women because women got humankind in trouble in the first place. And that still rides on women.

• • •

A woman cannot refuse a cesarean in this country. Women have been arrested in their homes and taken to the hospital in chains to give them a cesarean. Then if she lives in Tennessee—a state with no marital rape law—she can be impregnated against her will. Since Tennessee doesn't teach birth control in school, a woman can remain barefooted and pregnant all her childbearing life.

• • •

There are things done to women under the label "normal hospital procedure" but for which there's no medical evidence that the procedures do any good to anybody. Some of those things are:

Shaving women before they have babies. That doesn't help anything.

Episiotomies given routinely, which is to cut the woman a little bit. There's no reason for that. The midwives have shown that most women don't even tear. . . that the organism has evolved with a sufficient amount of evolutionary intelligence to stretch.

• • •

When I was a kid I once made a joke, saying, "Oh, this woman's hysterical, she ought to have a hysterectomy." Then I found out it wasn't a joke: The origin of the word "hysterectomy" comes from hysteria.

Women are having to endure things in hospitals that men don't. We don't, for instance, say about men, "This man's acting a little out of hand. . . let's cut his nuts off." They don't do things to men like that, but they do things to women like that routinely.

The problems those women given hysterectomies were having were maybe wanting to have their own money, or wanting to have a job outside of the home—which were considered mental illness. So then women had this drastic thing done to them—a hysterectomy—for opinions and attitudes that they had.

• • •

There ought to be an Equal Rights Amendment. If you don't have an Equal Rights Amendment, then people are going to chip away at whatever law you have. There needs to be an overarching law about equal rights for women, so that all insurance companies and all employers know that that is the law of the land.

There must be equal pay for equal work.

• • •

The Equal Rights Amendment is not an unreasonable thing to ask for, inasmuch as the country was not founded for the benefit of any women or black people. It was founded for the convenience of different kinds of white Protestant males.

• • •

I grew up with a pretty good set of regular sexist stuff. My parents were Marshall Dillon and Miss Kitty, just like *Gunsmoke*. It's not that at some point in my life I got cool, but that every once in a while some woman tells me that I'm in her territory—like when I'm talking to her I may be putting my hand on her. And I say, "Thank you. . . I hadn't noticed. I hadn't realized that." Sometimes it is just learning something new about the way women are treated, or hearing about the Taliban [in Afghanistan].

It is actually quite good when [women] tell you. It means they might keep on letting you hang around with them if you are good.

• • •

On the Farm, one of the things that was different about us from a lot of hippy stuff was that women got to say whether they got touched or not. They could say, "I don't want you to touch me," and you didn't get to argue about that.

We had pretty strict rules about being that way with women, and the result of it was that Farm ladies nursed freely in public and nobody gave them any crap about it. And the women were really grateful that they had that safe place to be, and often expressed their gratefulness.

• • •

Another Farm custom regarding women was this: If you're dating a single mother, you're courting the child, too.

• • •

One of the reasons the midwives were so successful on the Farm was because the men backed them up. If we only had one running truck on the Farm, it belonged to a midwife. And if a midwife called up a mechanic at three o'clock in the morning and said, "My truck won't start," he came out and started her truck for her.

• • •

Ms. magazine wrote a nice article about the Farm, saying that the Farm was something special for having created an atmosphere where a truly woman-based system of obstetrics could evolve.

The result of the Farm's woman-based approach was that our midwives had better birth mortality statistics than any hospitals in the United States. And they've had better birth mortality statistics than the 14 countries that are ahead of the United States.

• • •

Women's freedom is not just about wages. It's also about respecting women's energy. You don't get to act like you should have some of that energy if you're not in an agreed-on relationship with her.

If a woman's attitude is "I'd just as soon not be handled," then men don't get to come up and whip a big hug on her.

• • •

I stopped in London a couple of years ago on the way back from a speaking trip to Findhorn in Scotland. I was put up and fed and taken to various parties, houses, and clubs. It was lovely, being in London like a native, shopping with friends on Portobello Road for curry makings.

It was just after the Clarence Thomas hearings, and Anita Hill, I felt, had taken a low blow from Congress, and the Democrats didn't look much better than the Republicans about how they treated her.

When I landed in London, that was one of the first things that set off little bells. The men I talked to were very angry and judgmental about her and felt she was trying to screw up Clarence Thomas. That surprised me because I had watched maybe 16 hours of those hearings and she looked good to me. I even saw an autistic boy on TV who got hooked up with a computer so he could talk, and the first thing he said was, "I'm a Democrat and I believe Anita Hill!"

Later on at the dinner party (it was the curry we had shopped for), there were a lot of nice folks, English, kind of liberal people, who'd maybe been hippies when they were young. There was one fellow there who was very amusing, a good-looking man about 60 years old. I talked to him for quite a while and he was brilliant and fun to talk to and very witty. I had a great time with him. In fact, it's difficult to write this because I worry about losing his friendship. He had been a society photographer, the kind that went around to the fancy night clubs and took pictures of the rich and the famous folks during the '60s. The Beatles were hitting in England and he just got sucked into the action and became a hippy himself.

I talked with him for quite a while, turning on and drinking wine. And then, at a point, he took me over to the kitchen away from the women. He said he wanted to tell me something: "You know, it's funny. Whenever I drink and turn on at the same time, I get this terrible animosity towards women, and I feel like they have it towards me as well."

I thought, Oh, the poor guy's out of sorts with women, and I offered to help.

He didn't care at all for my offer of help, and went over and sat beside—and about half on—this much younger woman and started telling her about how women have this animosity about him and he couldn't help but notice all night long that she had this ill feeling toward him. She was a nice woman and her impulse was to try to ease him, but he ignored her protestations.

As I watched, I saw that it was absolutely a hoax. She hadn't had a speck of animosity toward him, but he did succeed in annoying her by pressing the issue. At that point I realized it was a ploy, a way to get into her energy and engage her juice.

It worked well.

Then he turned and did the same thing, with slight variations, to the next woman, and in a short time had the energy of all the women in this place tied up in this argument.

He ranged from very witty and doing Charlie Chaplin imitations to being downright nasty and beginning to assign hypothetical monetary values to people's hugs.

I was shocked, and I looked at the host, who was a friend, but he was letting it slide.

I tried to back the guy off a little bit by getting him into a discussion about Robert Bly's men's meetings. Bly says that there are a lot of men who were raised by single mothers or didn't have a man to grow up with, and he's saying that you can't learn to be a man from a woman. You have to learn to be a man from a man.

I mentioned that I had gone to a meeting like that once, not Robert Bly's personally, but one run by some people who were into his trip. When I listened to these men talk for a while, I felt like a spy. I felt like I was behind the lines under assumed colors because I don't feel out of sorts with women in general. I feel blessed in this way, because I have met the kind of women in my life who give you an introduction to being with a woman and let you know them in their hearts. This is where I disagree with Bly. I think you can learn how to be a man from a woman, and I think it might be one of the best places. I believe that if you ever actually know and love a woman, that's like being introduced to the whole species. You can love them all through that introduction.

Well, my friend at the party wasn't into any of those conversational gambits and tried to engage me on his side of the discussion by saying to me, "Isn't it true that women try to make men feel guilty more than men try to make women feel guilty?"

I said, "Actually, I have noticed that if you are nice to women and treat them humanly, you'll get some of that 'Oh, my hero!' kind of juice, which is really very nice and very rare."

He didn't know what I was talking about.

One of the women tried to translate: "He says if you're nice to them, they'll be nice to you!"

He ignored that as well. He couldn't afford to notice, because he got his energy from women by irritating and bugging them.

I didn't have any more leverage with him and I had been up since five o'clock that morning in Scotland, so I went to bed.

The next morning, having tea with my friend, I asked, "How come those women let that happen? Is that normal in England? Among people I know, a woman will defend herself."

These women even went so far as to call him a slob, but it had so much backwards English and politeness on it that it didn't faze him.

Later that morning one of the women at the party came over, and I asked her about it. At first she was polite and demurred, but then she revealed some anger and said, "Actually, he did use up all my time for the whole evening." I said that as long as he was able to keep his hooks into the energy, he would allow himself to be humiliated, laughed at, anything, as long as they didn't make him actually leave them alone. It reminded me of tripping times. The woman energy is much like the psychedelic energy and moves with many of the same dynamics. Undisciplined people can't resist trying to "steal" it.

Another similarity to the psychedelic dynamic is how much of the action is accomplished just above the awareness of the casual observer. When you see someone behaving in a fashion that is hard for you to understand, you have to look for the payoff.

Q: Why is this guy willing to accept humiliation from these women?

A: Because their attention is so precious—even given unwillingly—that it's worth enduring almost anything just to be into it.

When I see that Robert Bly can gather that big a club of men who haven't been introduced to women, I think there's something really wrong. These men were born out of women; they have sisters, a lot of them; they have interacted with a lot of women, from teachers to wives and girlfriends. What kept them from ever really hearing or meeting or understanding a woman? Some of it, I think, is fear of hearing what women really think.

It takes nerve to accept instruction from a woman. It's a spiritual and emotional contract. You say, "I'm going to be fair. I'm going to listen to you; I'm not going to use my size or my noise to run over you, and I'm going to trust you."

That's kind of like the Iroquois Confederacy—properly called the Haudenosaunee—whose chiefs are men, but who are chosen by women.

Can't you see a bunch of women sitting around and talking about a candidate for chief? One of them says, "I've been watching him since he was five years old, and he has been a bully on the playground all his life. This is not a chief!"

You have to realize that if a woman tells you something [negative], it doesn't mean that she hates you and that she is never going to have anything to do with you again. It might mean that maybe you were a nice person except for that glitch. That kind of stuff can frequently be very friendly, if you are smart enough to hear it.

I remember a time when I was in junior college and there were about 150 people in the coffee shop. This girl came up and said, in one loud, tearful tirade, "You may think that just because you are fast and smart and funny and can say things that cut people down that it's OK, and you think it's OK to do that, and that nobody cares, but I want you to know that somebody does care. I care!"

It didn't make me feel any better at all that I couldn't remember what I had said to her.

That girl taught me something.

When I was teaching at San Francisco State College, a young woman in one of my English classes felt the need to instruct me. "You think girls like you because of things you do or say, but you are wrong. There are other reasons that girls like you that don't have anything to do with that. The stuff you think girls like you for is mostly stuff that they just put up with, and they like you for stuff you don't even know about."

She was another woman who also had high standards about what a man was.

The one that left me the most thoughtful was later on, in my "just say thank you" days. I was waiting to come on and hanging out with the girl in the apartment upstairs. She was taking care of me and asked me a question about my previous love life and what it had been like. I talked to her for hours, about all the girls I had loved and lost and about not having any confidence about women and my worries about "manhood" and the sort of self-doubt that caused me to join the Marine Corps and to volunteer for combat overseas and to fall off motorcycles. I just generally spilled my soul to her. When I was done, she looked quizzically at me and said, "That's funny. I always thought a man was just the strongest, straightest, cleanest, bravest thing there ever was."

—*High Times* article

• • •

When I met my wife, she told me that I knew absolutely nothing about women but that she loved me anyway and if I would just shut up and be good, she would teach me. She asked what I thought she was in relation to me. I said, "It looks to me like you must be my teacher."

—*Paradigm Shift* magazine interview by Philip H. Farber, 1998

CHAPTER 15

Animal Rights

I'm amazed at people who can be cruel to animals, because it seems to me that if you pay any attention to them at all you see that they're really somebody.

You must enjoy dominating something to want to dominate animals.

I'm on two sides on the animal rights issue. On one side, I think there should be very strict enforcement of animal cruelty laws and the laws should be brought up to date, reflecting the new information we have about the intelligence and mental capabilities of animals.

That's on the legal side.

On the spiritual side, my dog friends, and cat friends, and horse friends are my friends. We recognize each other at a distance and they start coming to see me at the same time I start coming to see them. They're presences, and personages, and people. It's barbaric to treat them any other way.

• • •

We have this long-standing belief that we humans are higher forms of intelligence and higher on the food chain than animals so we should have dominion over them. But canaries are lower on the food chain than miners, but the miners value the role the canaries play in warning them about toxic air, and notice when they start falling down.

• • •

There's a 10 to one advantage to eating soybeans yourself rather than feeding them to a cow. It makes 10 times more protein for the world to eat the soybeans yourself instead of eating the cow that eats the soybeans.

We should think about that.

• • •

There's a way to do meat. If you're somebody who's not going to give up meat, you can think in terms of the way Third World countries use meat rather than eating 24-ounce steaks. In Oriental and Mexican cooking and Indian cooking it is mostly used as a garnish. I am not a weightlifter or a Ninja or anything like that. But I'm 65 years old and I have been a vegetarian for 35 years. My heart doctor says I have the heart of a teenager. I drive and read without eyeglasses.

I also eat my veggies.

• • •

Many cultures use animals as beasts of burden, and the animals don't do that work because they want to. But it all depends on where you live on the food chain. If somebody actually is making their living by plowing with a mule, I'm not going to get up in their business and tell them they can't plow with a mule.

I have the luxury of being pretty much a pacifist, because I live in the United States of America. If I lived in some Third World country, and my family was being killed, I'm not going to guarantee that I would be able to maintain a high-minded attitude.

I'm not going to judge the poor people who rebel against their treatment and don't have tractors but still have to grow their own crops. Moreover and most importantly, they're not the ones who're making the critters scarce.

We have a bunch of horses on the Farm and we did use them for some wagons and things like that when we were at that level of development. But they're still there, and they've raised generations of kids, and they're personages in their own right: Farm members.

• • •

I had a little monkey in my lap one time, and I had this horn which I was blowing. A cow horn. So I blew the horn and the monkey was fascinated. She took the horn away from me and tried to blow on it. I got her attention—puckered up my lips and blew out and showed her what I was doing with my mouth and put it on the horn. And she was so pleased that I showed her what it was she needed to know that she grabbed me around the head and kissed me. . . and loved me. . . and patted me.

• • •

When people are just barely surviving, I can't judge them for how they're doing it. When people live on a seacoast and fishing's the way their living is made, that's not my business.

The problem is that it's not all about family fishing anymore. It's about the factory fishers that go out and wipe out whole species of fish, and wipe out banks that have been fished at sustainable levels for hundreds of years.

That's part of the rape of the earth.

• • •

Frances Moore Lappé, who wrote *Diet for a Small Planet*, is a friend of mine. In her first book, she said that helping people feed themselves and be able to grow their own food is the thing. And this is a good diet that we have here in her book, which is mostly vegetarian and will not be hard on the earth and will return lots of food for hungry people.

And she did that for about 10 years.

Then on the cover of one of her later books, she said that for the last several years she'd been trying to do something about helping people to produce their own food and live adequately. And she'd come to find out over the years that if people were left alone, they'd already be feeding themselves adequately—and the reason they're not feeding themselves adequately and aren't able to take care of themselves on these levels is mostly because of the economic policies of the U.S.A. and the multinational corporations.

I agree with her, and I'm not going to judge the victims for how they have to live in order to make ends meet.

• • •

I don't see that we're going to get the whole world off of meat in any foreseeable future. But we've got to make the late-night TV comics quit making nasty faces over tofu.

We've made barbecued ribs out of tofu. When you freeze tofu, it gets tough and stringy and chewy. Freezing it also makes vacuoles in it as the water comes out of it, and those vacuoles really soak up the sauce. So we had some barbecue and were on a street in New York City and we gave some barbecue to this black dude that we were chatting with—we had the window of our bus open and we were eating right there. He had a few bites of it and said, "Where are the bones?"

CHAPTER 16

Gay Rights

There's much I could say about the many gay friends I've had and have and how much they've meant and taught to me. Perhaps the following, though, is all that I need to say for you to know why I feel specially friendly toward gay people and about protecting their rights.

Mother H.

I guess most people don't identify it with my hippy self, but I served with Able Company, First Battalion, Fifth Marine Regiment in Korea in 1953 as a rifleman, a Browning automatic rifleman, and a fire-team leader. I drew combat pay and was fired on and returned fire and carried dead and wounded friends back from no man's land.

All this talk about gays in the military took me back 40 years to those times. We had several combat corpsmen, the Marine Corps name for a medic, in our company but the most memorable was Mother H.

Mother H. was about six feet four and handsome with close-cut, black, curly hair, a fine-looking young man who wanted nothing more than to resume his homosexual life back in San Francisco. Our platoon thought it was pretty slick to have a gay corpsman. We thought we got good treatment, Mother H. was kind and compassionate and we felt we were covered. Mother H. obviously cared for us and that gentleness was much appreciated in those hard combat situations. To my knowledge, he never "hit on" any of us.

Mother was good on patrols. One time we went out not long after full dark. We entered no man's land through the Panmunjom "Peace Corridor" with its red and white, candy-striped guard shack with the guard in his spiffy white gloves, white spats, white duty-belt, and chrome helmet. We were quite a contrast in our camouflage and blackened faces. After a few hundred yards we left the peace corridor and turned toward Three Fingers and Horseshoe, Chinese-held hills. We managed to penetrate fairly deeply into Chinese territory without alerting any sentries and, having completed our mission, turned back toward our own lines, looking for the sally gate where we could re-enter our lines.

There was a trench all the way across Korea, roughly at the 38th parallel. First there was a row of trenches with fighting holes and machine gun bunkers every few yards, then a 30-foot-wide strip of tanglefoot barbed wire five feet deep, mined with occasional trip flares. Outside the barbed wire was our mine field. Some of the mines would blow a man up. Some would blow up a tank.

The mine field, for the safety of the U.N. forces, had one strand of barbed wire running down our side of the field with a small red triangle hanging every few feet. On the posts facing our line were signs: WARNING, MINE FIELD.

As we hunted the sally gate, we ran up against the one-strand fence, saw the triangles, and read the sign, upside down from the wrong side. We had been led across the mine field and were standing in it.

We, of course, wanted to be on the other side of that fence and started to step over when the sergeant, who had led us into the mine field, said, "No. We made it this far. We're going to turn around and retrace our steps through the field, go back and re-enter through the peace corridor."

Opinions flared, whether to cross out of the mine field or go back through it, when suddenly Mother H. drew his .45, jacked back the slide, and pointed it at the sergeant. "Sergeant," he said, "this appears to me to be a health question. I'm in charge of health and it looks unhealthy to the men to go back through that mine field after we were lucky enough to make it the first time. We're going to step over the fence and go in through the sally port. You can run me up on charges when we get back to our own company area, but that's what we are going to do now."

The sergeant looked down the barrel of the .45 and reluctantly agreed.

In the morning we all waited on tenterhooks for the sergeant and Mother H. to tell their stories to the captain. We feared for Mother's safety. There were dark rumors that people who misbehaved in combat could be stood up against the wall and shot. When Mother came back down the hill, we were all over him.

"Well, what happened?"

Mother smiled.

"Nothing, to me."

"What happened to the sergeant?"

Mother smiled more broadly.

"He was relieved of duty as a squad leader and sent to the rear to be a cook."

That was one of the best good-sense decisions I ever saw come down through the official channels of the Marine Corps.

We all thought, "Mother takes good care of us!"

CHAPTER 17

The Family

I believe that there's kind of an equation that the amount of oppression that comes from the government downward through the population is translated into intramural violence among fragments of the population: and among men and women, and so on.

It's like, you can't fight City Hall, but you can kick your wife. . . she's a lot smaller. . . and defenseless.

We're at a point, now, where people are afraid to be parents to their own kids. They're afraid to hug a kid. We've got so much craziness going on and people going to the law courts.

• • •

On the Farm we've had our own schools. Most of the kids of the early generations of the Farm went to the Farm school at least up to mid–high school. My children did. It wasn't home schooling, though we have that now. Today, some members of the Farm send their kids to public schools, some engage in home school, and some send their kids to the Farm school.

Most of the teachers in the Farm school have been parents, and the school has been accredited by the State of Tennessee. In Tennessee, if you have a qualified teacher who's been to college, that teacher can deputize teachers under their credentials to work and teach. We didn't have any quarrels in the state with our school, because we had so many college-educated people. In fact, at one time, the Farm had more college degrees than the Tennessee legislature did.

• • •

If your baby doesn't want anything to do with you, one of you is on an ego trip, you or the baby. (If your baby doesn't want anything to do with you, then by far you are the more likely culprit.)

If a baby has been distracted by its parents as a method of control, it can learn it doesn't have to pay attention to anybody, and it won't.

If you're going to learn how to deal with kids, you've got to learn how to come on strong without a bad vibe. Don't think that you have to come on nasty. But you might have to come on strong—without any bad vibes, without any anger, without any guilt, without any blame—just a little noise, kid, to attract your attention. Then you have to reason with the kid. At that point, it's also good to remember that you don't want your kids to learn that they should just knuckle under to strong juice.

—"Monday Night Class, The New Edition" (unpublished)

• • •

The idea is that you want your kids to know which way is up. If you stay in one-to-one, truthful contact with them by telling them honestly what it is that they're doing, and how it is that it affects you, honestly, all the time, then when they're 15 or 16 years old, they're not strangers; they're still your friends, they know what's happening. . . . [But] that means you're gonna have to point which way is up, and keep pointin' that way until they catch on.

—*Monday Night Class*

• • •

Anybody who wants to sit around a baby and look at him and pay attention to him can get high.

—*Monday Night Class*

• • •

Part of the way to protect poor kids so they get a proper education and chance in life is if we just implement programs, [which were] implemented a long time ago, that the Republicans have chipped away at. The Republicans tried to stop Head Start, which is a very important program. They tried to stop help for inner-city schools— they want to do vouchers and fund white flight so white people can all run away from black people, and then the black people don't get quality schools.

• • •

Here in Tennessee, we have some of the best highways in the United States. . . yet the plaster is falling off some of the school rooms in Nashville.

There's no air-conditioning in those buildings. Sometimes they have to let school out [when it's too hot to be inside].

• • •

Kids are smart. They know when they're getting the short end of the stick. . . and it doesn't make them be good citizens.

People that you abuse do not become good citizens.

• • •

Responsibility means "ability to respond." A child can grab off a larger chunk of free will than he or she is physically or intellectually capable of being responsible for. That means that a parent is responsible for the child's karma. It's like that thing about the cat: You can let go of a cat and it'll land on its feet. But you can throw a cat so hard that it can't land on its feet. Then it's not its own cat anymore, it's "your" cat.

Well, the same thing applies to a kid. You don't give a kid the chance to decide whether to drink rat poison or not. A kid has free will, and can decide whether to drink a bottle of rat poison or not, but you don't give a kid who doesn't know any better the chance to make that mistake.

It's that way with a whole lot of things relating to kids. If a kid gets to where he can't pay attention to you, because you've lost his attention, then his attention's just wandering, out in the universe, and will fasten on any piece of interesting stuff that goes by—and then it's off to the races, on a randomly programmed [course].

I've seen a kid who never had any attention paid to him, and it was like nobody had ever reached out and grabbed on. The kid was just flopping. It took a long time and quite a bit of work to be able to just get the kid's attention enough to say hello—to say, "Are you there? Are you inside there? What's happening?"

I know grownups like that, too. Nobody ever managed to get their attention, and so their attention belongs to whatever billboard is beside the freeway, especially if it's painted day-glo. Their minds belong to whatever professional mind-copper can cop them. If you don't know where your attention is, then you're wide open to having your head copped by anybody who can cop a head. I mean specifically the advertising industry, politicians, gurus, college "experts," et cetera.

—"Monday Night Class, The New Edition" (unpublished)

• • •

I don't think that the federal government should dictate education, but the federal government should dictate that there is education for everyone in the entire country.

CHAPTER 18

Environment

I hope it's not too mystical for people to know that I think that the earth and its inhabitants are a great biological system. . . and if you harm any part of it, you harm the whole thing.

For the first time, today, we've been able to prove that smog makes it not rain. We have the figures, the facts, the satellite mapping—areas that don't have pollution have normal historical rainfall for those areas. Areas that have pollution, the rain doesn't fall on them. The reason is that rain condenses around dust particles. We have so much particulates, though, that there's not enough water to go around and coat them all and raindrops don't get heavy enough to fall.

• • •

Here we are globally killing the last of our fish and big mammals. We're hunting out our whales and we're hunting out our salmon, and we're blocking up the rivers that salmon live in. And the ice pack is melting.

I have half of my winter's firewood sitting out in my yard right now, because winter's over and I don't need any more firewood because the winter isn't lasting so long.

There are large portions of the population—quite likely a majority of the world's population—that understand this and don't like it. And they can't do anything about it, because the courts are stacked, the laws are stacked, the sovereignty is stacked, the media is stacked. . . right down the line.

• • •

Jimmy Carter said that what should be done about the energy crisis is the moral equivalent of war. And he was absolutely correct—and he's the best President in my lifetime.

• • •

I think the federal government should use the power of eminent domain and protect every redwood forest in the United States, making them national parks. If the forests were on someone's property, give that person fair market value of that property before it was set aside as a national park.

• • •

Issues like the one they had in the Northwest about making a choice between preserving the spotted owl nests or preserving the lumber workers' jobs and cutting down the forests where the owls live are false dichotomies that are set up on purpose by corporations. There's no reason for people to think they'll be unemployable and out of work because they can't cut down old-growth timber. The workers were given a false sense of the options. They were told, "Cut down spotted owl nest trees or don't work, lose your jobs." They weren't told that they had another choice: Cut down owl nest trees and destroy the owls' nests. . . or have this other job over here using similar equipment and doing work that actually needs to be done.

There is a lot of stuff in this country that needs to be done and we need someone with the vision of Roosevelt to create the necessary jobs.

• • •

We could have a Roosevelt CCC—Civilian Conservation Corps— where people go out and clean out Superfund sites. The only reason the Republicans don't want to do this is that some of the people who dirtied up the sites would have to pay for them. Republicans consider it an infringement on their freedom that they should have to bury their own poop.

• • •

The trouble with the real hard-core, capitalist, private-property lick is that it doesn't recognize the foolishness of putting a fence around something: Nobody who lives 100 years owns a redwood tree that lives 3,000 years.

That's an amusing conceit on their part.

• • •

There're things that are so grand and so great and so beautiful that they don't even belong to countries.

Such as the redwood trees.

I think the redwood trees should be an international park, and no country should have the right to make any law that would ever harm them.

• • •

In my travels I discovered that the Gold Rush that hit California and the guys who cut the redwoods were really part of an international trend. They did the same thing to New Zealand: Gold Rush and cut the big trees; same thing in Australia: Gold Rush and cut the big trees.

I went to museums in New Zealand and Australia and saw this one place where they would dam up a canyon, run a lake in it, and fill it up with trees. . . and then pull the plug and let the dam break. And let millions of gallons of water and millions of tons of trees tear down a valley, ripping everything out to the subsoil, all the way to the bottom, to transport their trees. . . destroying maybe 10 miles of canyon each time.

They did the same excessive gold mining down there as they did here. That was an international effort: The Gold Rush was an international effort, and so was the tree cut.

Now this thing has to be handled world-wide, through the United Nations. But I don't know if the United Nations is going to survive or not—because it's got down to where there are the atomic powers and the poor people. The poor people pass a lot of laws, and the atomic powers all have the veto and don't let them have them.

• • •

The gasoline and the automobile companies continued to pump lead into the environment. . . although all these years you could go to college and learn that the fall of the Roman Empire was partly on account of lead pipes.

Stephen and Garrick Beck, Rainbow Farm, Oregon.

CHAPTER 19

Gun Control

**We have too many guns in our society.
Rage venting itself on someone, without a weapon,
can usually wear itself out before the other person is dead.**

John Wayne and Charlton Heston are movie actors; I am a Marine Corps combat veteran.

I served with Able Company, First Battalion, Fifth Marine Regiment, First Marine Division, in Korea in 1953 as a rifleman, Browning automatic rifleman, fire-team leader, and acting squad leader. I drew combat pay and was fired on and returned fire and carried dead and wounded friends back from no man's land in the rice paddies.

I was a good shot at 18. With the M1 rifle I was able to put 10 shots out of 10 into a 20-inch bull's-eye at 500 yards. With the Thompson submachine gun, the M2 carbine, and the A-6 machine gun, I could fire off one shot at a time while set on fully automatic and I was very accurate firing bursts of two and three from the hip. I tell you all this so you will know that I know what I am talking about when I say that it is self-evident that fully automatic weapons loose in the general population is insanity. Automatic weapons' only purpose is for killing people.

I grew up in a house with guns, not "weapons." My father was a sportsman who owned and appreciated fine guns that were kept in a locked case. My favorite was a 25/35, octagonal, long-barreled model 1894 Winchester. It could have been displayed in an art museum. It had the cleanness of a Brancusi sculpture. I tell you this part so you will know that I don't think we should be taking people's hunting rifles and target guns.

My own gun was a Remington single-shot, bolt-action .22. My father wouldn't let me have a .22 that was a repeater. He said that if I could just shoot a bunch of times in a row, that I never would learn to be a careful shot.

I think that if the police officers who shot at [Amadou] Diallo 41 times had been trained by my father, Diallo would still be alive.

One of the causes of no-knock search and other constitutional illegalities, such as the Diallo killing, is the very real fear on the part of police who have to work in an environment full of guns. The police don't want to see everyone armed. Things are tough enough as it is. This fear is why cops are taught, on the pistol range, to empty their weapons at someone. If they were careful shots, like my father taught, they would be good enough shots to shoot someone in the leg and maybe not have to blow every suspect clear away.

The NRA does not represent law enforcement. The NRA does not care so much about people owning guns as it does about corporations being able to sell guns. The NRA interpretation of the Second Amendment is simplistic and disingenuous. When the government wanted everyone to have a gun, in the Revolutionary War era, it was because guns were very expensive, rare, and "high tech." Only about one man in 10 even had one. When they conscripted troops in those times, they were expected to bring their own guns. The clue to the intent of the Amendment is the part about the "well-trained militia." It is not about the right of every disgruntled, drunken yahoo to own a terrorist's wet dream, fully automatic, machine pistol.

There are currently three private guns for every man in the U.S.A., or more than enough guns for every man, woman, and child to have one. We do not have a gun shortage problem.

In many ways, the problem is not even guns. The problem revolves more around lobbyists, legislators, and money.

I am sure that many of these problems would be solvable if we didn't have to fight the NRA lobby to get safe gun laws.

We could do something about tobacco if we didn't have to fight the tobacco lobby.

We might do better with our children if we didn't have to fight the Ritalin/Prozac lobby.

There is nothing unreasonable in the Brady law. With the passage of this law:

- Requiring background checks and waiting periods for handgun purchases has kept more than 300,000 handguns out of the wrong hands as a result.
- A federal assault weapons ban and six state assault weapons bans have passed.
- The national ban on "cop-killer" bullets has passed.
- The national ban on plastic handguns has passed.
- Child access prevention laws have passed in 16 states.
- Comprehensive, precedent-setting gun laws have passed in Connecticut, Hawaii, Massachusetts, and Maryland.
- So far, the NRA's concealed weapons bills in Congress have been blocked.

The Center to Prevent Handgun Violence continues to defend these laws in court against NRA-backed challenges.

In order to make the Brady law even more effective, the following should be passed right away:

- Require the licensing of every handgun owner.
- Require the registration of every handgun.
- Ban importation of high-capacity ammunition magazines.
- Require safety locks to be sold with all guns.
- Prohibit the sale or transfer of assault rifles to children under the age of 18.
- Close the gun-show loophole.

The Republicans and the Libertarians are wrong. There is a reason to have a strong government. The government's role should be fighting to protect the rights of the people in a heartless market economy instead of accepting money from lobbyists to sell out the public interest.

That's the sense of the whole thing: Guns have been considered a consumer product, rather than as a weapon with karma hanging on every molecule. The NRA cannot tell the difference as "products" between a fried pie and a pistol.

• • •

I'm a vegetarian, but I haven't got anything particularly against someone going out and hunting for food. We ask the neighbors not to hunt on our property, because our children horseback ride all over our property. And mostly they respect that.

Sometimes during deer-hunting season, out-of-town people come through, and we have to run them off our property. But the neighbors respect us. And we've achieved that without having any guns.

We have also not been naive in that although we do not have any guns ourselves, we took a collection (taxes) and hired (elected) this fellow with a gun to protect us. We call him the sheriff.

• • •

Firing your pistol 17 times, like with your Glock—bang, bang, bang, bang, bang—is a product of fear. And that fear is from living in a society that's stuffed with guns. It scares the police and makes the police dangerous: The cops will drop you, man, for reaching for your wallet.

When the cops are running in fear of their lives because of so many guns in our society, then we are in an escalating arms race.

• • •

Some little town in Mississippi—I forget the name of it, but I saw it on television—said that they couldn't afford to be without special weapons, and they couldn't afford to be out-gunned by the criminals. And they had voted a city bond to buy the cops a Heckler-Koch 850-round-a-minute machine gun. . . for some little town where the chief crime is speeding teenagers.

• • •

The cops have special powers about dope, they've got special powers about guns, they've got special powers about search and seizure, they've got special powers about no-knock. . . and so now we've got an incredibly militarized armed police force.

When I lived in San Francisco, the cops wore suit coats, their guns were inside their coats, and they wore soft-top hats.

When I left San Francisco, they wore motorcycle riding pants, high black boots, heavy-weight pistol rigs. . . with their mace and their clubs and their tazer all hanging on their belts, and their handcuffs, and their plastic helmets, and their mirror shades.

And I watched the demonstrations that got violent turn the cops from cops to troops.

• • •

Back in World War II, the medics in the field didn't carry weapons. There was a set of agreements made between all the civilized countries of the world, called the Geneva Convention, and it was agreed that medics wouldn't carry weapons, and that nobody would fire on them. Then we got into some real ugly race wars, where we hated the Japanese for being Japanese, and we hated Germans for being German, and the Germans hated us for being Americans, and we all got into a lot of hate, and we began to pick off each other's ambulances. We began to shoot at each other's medics. Medics began to carry weapons.

By the time I got to Korea, when I was on line in combat, the medics all carried pistols. By Vietnam, the medics all carried automatic weapons. In modern warfare, we had given up respect for the medics.

There is a young priest in Quiche province in Guatemala, where much of the violence has been going on. This young priest used to be in the Irish Republican Army, the I.R.A. Now he is a priest in Quiche. He serves Mass. They have a picture in the newspaper of him with a [Communion] wafer in his hand, with a little altar. He's radical, and he talks radical, and he has to sleep in a different place every night, because he knows there's a hit list out on him. Somebody wants to kill him. He has decided what kind of an example he's going to be to the Indians. He keeps a .357 magnum pistol under his Bible. He said the Archbishop of El Salvador was shot down at Mass. He says he's going to go down fighting; he thinks it's an example to the Indians for him to go down fighting.

That's really a tragic story. A dude with that kind of courage could set a better example. And the result of the example he sets is that it's open season on priests. They'll say, "A priest might have a gun."

Every time civilization slips and loses that respect, all of mankind is a little less civilized. We've all slipped back toward the carnivores. I can't tell that priest to stay in Quiche and get killed any more than I could tell our Plenty crew in Solola that they had to stay there when it was dangerous. But our guys were down there and they weren't carrying guns. They were pretty safe down there because nobody was mad at them. They hadn't been trying to do anything wrong to the people. They hadn't been being rich gringos, and they had been trying to help the people out.

I used to think it was a terrible mistake that I went in the Marine Corps. But I don't feel that way now. I want to be somebody who went to combat and carried weapons and was even shot at, who didn't kill nobody, and ain't gonna and don't wanna. I won't carry a gun. I'll carry the state of the art in radio, and whatever makes us fast and smart and able to move quickly—I'll go for all that; but I don't want to carry anything for hurting some other people.

—*Rendered Infamous*

• • •

The point is that in our day and age, we're not going to duke it out with the government with hand weapons. That's ridiculous; it's just not going to happen.

And if you do have a bunch of guns, you find out what it's going to be like.

Look at the [Symbionese Liberation Army], the MOVE commune, and Waco.

When the government found out the SLA was well-armed, that was the first time we saw military-level bazookas and crap happening in a suburb of the United States. Suddenly we had Vietnam-level weapons in the suburbs. And at the same time that was happening, the television series *The A-Team* was softening everybody up for military-level weapons in the suburbs, too.

You can't run a society where you have random caches of military-level stuff around.

• • •

I don't think that the issue is even about sporting weapons. That's not a problem, so much. The problem is about what used to be called "Saturday night specials"—cheap pistols that are about nothing but intimidating.

• • •

In England, it was not common for people to carry guns. The cops didn't even go armed. The Bobbies had sticks—they didn't carry guns. And the criminals didn't carry guns. It was not a gun trip.

As soon as it's a gun trip, you're not going to keep the bad guys from having guns.

• • •

We license people to drive cars, and we have real stiff controls about how and when and where you use your car. . . or they take your driver's license away.

Why isn't it the same way with guns?

• • •

I was raised with guns all my life. My father had guns; all my uncles had guns on my father's side of the family. On my mother's side of the family, my great-grandfather, who was a prospector, was a U.S. Marshal and he had a gun.

I saw someone wrote just recently that there is a rite of passage about guns. Somewhere around 12 years old, they let you have a gun. I remember firing a heavy 12-gauge shotgun when I was about 10, which recoiled itself completely out of my grasp onto the ground when I fired it. When I was 12, I got a .22 rifle; my father bought me a single-shot. He said that automatic rifles are for poor shots. If you have a single-shot rifle, you'll learn to be a better shot, because you have to make the first one count. I remember on many occasions firing on a running rabbit, and missing the first time, and never having a second chance. I'm not sure if my father's advice made me a better shot, but it saved the lives of many rabbits.

I only actually initiated one hunt on my own that was a successful hunt. It was not large, but the impact was sufficient. I was 14 years old or so, living in Santa Fe, New Mexico, in the wintertime with six or eight inches of snow on the ground. I was home with the winter flu, and was wishing for something to do.

I glanced out the window and saw a large bluebird sitting on top of the telephone pole 50 or 60 feet from the door of our house.

I picked up my BB gun, my trusty Daisy, cranked the lever, and stepped out the door briefly in my bathrobe and slippers. I carelessly threw the BB gun to my shoulder and dropped the bluebird with one shot.

I was sick. I hadn't the slightest idea that I might hit him. I thought I might rattle the cables near him, drive him away, or scare him, but my casual unthinking marksmanship was clean as Zen, and very deadly; it dropped the bluebird in the snow.

—*Rendered Infamous*

• • •

The only weapon I didn't do well with was the .45 pistol. Its kick was so violent, and it was so loud, and it bruised my wrist so severely, that by the end of a day's target practice I would have to squeeze to avoid losing the gun. I would send a series of shots off up in the air before I could get control of it enough to make it stop shooting in my hand.

In Korea, whenever I was in combat situations, I always seemed to lose my gun and carry stretchers. My entire lifetime's accumulation of reading adventure stories and training with weapons was completely lost and useless to me the first time I saw someone shot. I could think of nothing in the world more important than to help that person who was shot; the idea of shooting still more people seemed unthinkable to me, even in the heat of combat. It would be like seeing a car wreck and hurting the people some more. . . .

• • •

I am not paranoid about guns. But from my viewpoint, I want to say that a gun may not cause violence, but guns cause death. To continue to sell an unlimited supply of all the guns you want into a culture that is propagandized many hours a day by television and movies that it is somehow all right or normal to kill, is to create a situation where crime will be, possibly not more prevalent, but much more deadly. Even a fit of rage, one person venting his rage fully on another person, beating him into insensibility, probably won't cause more damage than can be healed in a couple of weeks. But if there is a weapon in the situation, a moment's whim can be accomplished in a second's action. The human being is not easy to kill. But a gun makes it easy. That is wrong. That is a wrongness loosed on society in the name of production and commerce and profit. I don't think it is possible or practical to go collect up all the guns in our society. There are, I am sure, hundreds of thousands of people like my father who, although they have a veritable arsenal stashed away somewhere in their house, are not violent people, and are not made violent by owning guns; but I do know that the country has a love affair with the gun, from the Colt Peacemaker to the .45 to the Derringer to the Saturday night special.

• • •

When I was in Canada recently, I was asked, "Why do Americans have all those guns?"

My first answer was, "I don't have any."

But I was not allowed this easy cop-out. I had to answer for Americans and their guns, whether I had any or not.

They said, "You have 50 thousand guns down there."

I said, "That's not nearly as many as we have down there."

Sure enough, when I saw the article they'd read, it was 50 million guns, not 50 thousand.

I had to explain to the Canadians why the Constitution said we could have guns. They did not understand. It was amusing when I pointed out to them that the reason the Constitution said we could have guns was so the British couldn't come and take us back. It stopped the audience cold. They were stunned and thoughtful as they considered that. . . those who still live under a monarchy.

Circumstances alter cases and time alters circumstances. We are not going to defend ourselves from the British coming to get us, or the Russians, or anyone else, with a bunch of sporting rifles and pistols. It is not on this level that the battle is joined. It is an illusion to convince the people that they are safer from foreign aggression because they have a bunch of rifles and pistols. Their rifles and pistols and their laughably small sporting supply of ammunition, as compared with a wartime supply of ammunition, are strategically unimportant in a modern war.

Some Americans have reason to fear the Saturday night special. But many more Americans have reason to fear the cruise missile, the intercontinental ballistic missile, the MX missile, the multiplying-target re-entry vehicle missile, the neutron bomb; all are much more potentially deadly than the Winchesters and Remingtons and Colts and Smith & Wessons floating around in our culture. Handguns are a symbol of sickness; they are a symptom. But they are not the disease. The disease is far more deadly than they are.

I don't think registration and licensing is unreasonable. The National Rifle Association tells us that registration and licensing would make it hard for people to have guns. We register and license automobiles, and everybody has one. When an automobile is used in the commission of a crime, we can sometimes see what its plates are, and its [owner's] registration has a description, which can aid us to find and track that person down. It would [be] the same thing with a gun; it is not unreasonable to consider the registration and licensing of handguns.

I know that some people will think I am right-wing or soft on guns because I don't advocate a more punitive or restrictive path. But I don't think a question of this material plane magnitude can be attacked without material plane considerations. Once again, the question arises of who is the criminal: the undereducated, undertrained, laid-off, unemployed holdup man with the .38 in his

hand, or the clean, well-bathed, sweet-smelling executive somewhere in his drawing room, who made and sold millions of them
for business?

We have multinational corporations selling weapons around
the world. Phillip Habib is shuttling between Israel and Lebanon
trying to make peace, and we have a large number of salesmen
from Lockheed, Rockwell, Boeing, Grumman, trying to sell them
the stuff to make war with, while Habib is one guy trying to get
them to stop.

Years ago, owning a Thompson submachine gun was a federal
offense which would put the FBI on your front doorstep immediately. Now, every paramilitary movement carries automatic
weapons that should be illegal at a federal level, and the presence of
these weapons is somehow seen as less of a threat than a few inch-
and-a-half-barrel, .32 six-shooters floating around the inner city.

The automatic weapons in the paramilitary groups already
have strong laws forbidding their [ownership by] the general public; and if these laws were enforced at the level they should be enforced, many citizens would feel less paranoia in their lives, and
possibly less reason to own a handgun.

I don't like to see the right wing arming themselves and organizing paramilitary groups; I also don't like to see the Jews arming
themselves and organizing as a paramilitary group; and I also don't
like to see any hippy survivalists arming themselves and organizing
as a paramilitary group. I don't want to see any black people buying
guns and organizing as a paramilitary group. I don't want anybody
to do that. I will defend anyone's right to their opinions, but I am not
willing to defend anyone's guns.

—Rendered Infamous

CHAPTER 20

Yard Goods

Activism

A lot of people should do the kind of things I'm doing.

We should join together with people of a like mind who have any juice or any power to do anything at all. We have to get to where there's enough of us together in a large voting body that somebody cares about what we think.

And they don't, currently.

• • •

I've been exposed to that kind of stuff [activism, social consciousness] since my youth, and it may have made its mark on me. My grandmother was a suffragette, and was in the streets for the women's vote. I saw a picture of her in her suffragette suit, which was pretty severe. She always wore pants and slacks and stuff well after many of her daughters were pretty wealthy and moved in pretty high social [circles]. She made her own pantsuits and said, "I wear pants."

—*Rendered Infamous*, p. 7

Aging

On my being 65: The bones may squeak, but the electricity still goes at the speed of light.

• • •

The Zen master told of an old Zen blessing:

Grandfather die,
Father die,
Son die.

The student asked, "What the hell kind of blessing is that?"
Replied the Zen master: "It's in the right order."

• • •

In her eighties, my grandmother said, "Old age ain't so bad when
you consider the alternative."

Attention

Attention is energy.
   What you put your attention on, you get more of. Each one of us
is a fountain of energy, a valve through which universal life energy
is metered into the world, and we can each point our self at whatever we want to. We add life force to our surroundings—to everything we pay attention to. If you put your attention on the best, highest, finest, most beautiful thing that you can, that will be amplified.

                                                    —*This Season's People*, p. 29

Big Brother

I got something by e-mail recently and I looked at it and thought,
Man, this looks like somebody's paranoid fantasy to me. It was
about something called Echelon—a code name for a complex of
satellites equipped with decoding technology.
   What it's about—and it's now surfacing in the media and it's
true and it's real—is that there exists a spy network that can read
every phone call, every fax. . . everything that passes on a satellite
in the world. And we've got them stashed in Finland, and England, and every place. . . all around the world.

The e-mail I got told of a guy who'd told a woman friend of his that he'd show her what you could do with this network. He punched up some numbers, and she recognized this voice. This friend of hers had walked right into a phone call of Strom Thurmond's. He'd gotten into the Senate Office Building and into Strom Thurmond's office and was listening to Thurmond talk.

And her friend was in northern England!

Another woman then got her own name on the Echelon list because in a phone conversation with a friend, she said that her son's play at school had "bombed," and the use of that word triggered the satellite and got her on the list.

The U.S.A. and its allies own Echelon. It was originally put together for interdicting Russians to monitor what they were buying.

Capital Punishment

There're people who are too untrustworthy to be ever let loose into the population, and whether they were dead or not wouldn't make much of a difference—except for the problem that the State is neither wise enough, nor honest enough, nor unracist enough to be making those kinds of decisions.

And certainly no one else if not the State.

Church

The Church, under the guise of spirit, has gotten more and more into guiding the flesh.

Collectives and Communes

The prototype of the little collectives were the bands—like The Holding Company and the Jefferson Airplane. Because the bands were something that had a means of production and certain necessities that they had to be into—a certain level of electronic and other competence.

The band showed people that you could get together as an entity that could help each other out.

Then kids figured out that you didn't have to do music in order to be that sort of entity.

• • •

Sometimes I've said that the United States has become like a freeway, and if you go walking out on the freeway as a person with the semi-tractor trailer rigs from the corporations and stuff, they'll just run over you. So what you have to do is get together with a bunch of other persons and put a big vehicle of your own on the freeway.

Communication

If you want to communicate with people, you have to work at it all the time, every waking minute. You have to work at it really hard, because many people are afraid.

If you think you've done enough when you do 50 percent of the work, that won't make it, because to touch some people you may have to do 100 percent of the work. You can't ever say, "Well, I've tried hard enough." You have to keep on trying and keep on trying, remembering that folks really do want to be touched. They really do want to be communicated with.

—*This Season's People*, p. 63

Drug Dealers

There was some guy who got into quite a bit of trouble for pointing out that the coke dealers were actually some of the best entrepreneurs in the community.

But dealing was the only business they could get into without a bank loan.

• • •

As long as money is involved with cocaine, and as long as money is involved with heroin, and as long as money is involved with marijuana, they will be unmanageable.

Elderly and Disabled

For old folks and disabled folks, the government should fund bureaus and agencies to take care of these people that are staffed by these people. Because they will know what they need.

Like the guy who speaks for the disabled vets was a wheelchair guy, and the vets liked that quite a lot.

The people who are trying to figure out how to get employment for people who can't work 40-hour weeks and have to have some kind of special way they can work. . . well, let the people who have to have a special way they can work have the job of figuring out how to do it.

Forgiveness

If you've been hassling your friends or your family and then you decide you have to straighten up, then you really do have to go to each one of them that you had a hassle with and get straight with them. "Straight with them" is when you feel right with them, not when you give them a present or anything like that, but when you feel straight with them. You have to get that way with each of them, and that cancels all the bad vibrations that you put into those folks, because we have the power of forgiveness, which is a heavy power. By forgiveness you can take the evil out of bad deeds.

—*The Caravan*

• • •

Forgiveness is another kind of thing [than blame]. If somebody came along and [stole something from you], and then later on down the line they got caught and somebody says, "Hey, I caught this fellow that took your thing, what should I do to him?" and you think, Wow, I don't want to do anything to him, what you can say is, "I give it to him now retroactively. I fore-give him." Ain't that neat? You say, "It's okay, you could have had my permission."

—*The Caravan*

• • •

If you've already done [something that causes another pain], then what you have to do is straighten up and groove in the here and now—same instructions all the time. As soon as you get done doing something dumb, straighten up and groove in the here and now. That's how you can get it back. You have to learn how to forgive yourself at a place like that and say "OK." It's not that you can't blow it—free will implies that you can blow it. The heavy thing is that you can always get it back.

—*The Caravan*

G.I. Bill

I think the G.I. Bill was one of the greatest things this country ever did. My family was not about to pay for me going to college. I got to go to college because I went into the Marine Corps and got the G.I. Bill.

When I got out of the Marines, I asked, "What are the hippest schools in the country?" I was told, Antioch, and Reed, and The New School in New York, and San Francisco State College. And San Francisco State College cost $79 a semester. Not a unit, a semester. All of it. And my G.I. Bill paid $135 a month, because I was married.

And I thought, Man, I'm in tall cotton. I get to go to one of the four hippest schools in the country for $79. And San Francisco State College was very well regarded. Nobody held it against them that it was 79 bucks a semester.

And, of course, a lot of things happened there that I might not have gotten at Reed: I got to be in the cradle of it and have my mind taken over by the hippies.

Government

I'm not for limited government, necessarily. I think we should have the amount of government that it takes to do the job.

Occam's razor says that entities must not be multiplied beyond necessity.

I believe in that.

But you can't leave out anything that it takes to make the machine work, either. And society is supposed to be a clean-running machine.

• • •

The role of the federal government should be to provide all people the opportunity to be the best they can possibly be. And the things that are provided should not be for profit.

If those things are for profit, then who are we ripping off? The future generations we're trying to educate and provide for.

• • •

The government is basically a machine. It is something whose parts are made of laws and rules instead of levers and wires. But it's a machine.

A corporation is a machine, too.

And a machine should do nothing but serve you. A machine has no reason for existing but to serve you. There's no reason to build a machine that doesn't serve you.

A machine that's not good for people, that's not good for humankind, is a waste of resources to build.

• • •

Republicans talk about Big Government, but Big Government doesn't hurt us. Big Military hurts us. Big corporations with price fixing hurt us.

Everyone who thinks that they are being robbed because they should pay for some of the roads they drive on is not quite able to understand that it's the government that connects their driveways.

I love driving my little car on the freeway system. . . and I didn't have anything to do with that except pay my gasoline taxes.

Here-and-Now

Keep your attention in the here-and-now. Don't past-trip. Putting your attention in the past means that here-and-now is continuing on without you. The more time you spend in the past, the farther and farther out of register you are.

Don't put your attention into the future, other than a reasonable amount of plans that you intend to carry out. Putting your attention out into the future is like when a squirrel runs out on a tree limb—when he gets way out into the small limbs, it gets very shaky. When you get out into the thin possibilities, it gets very unlikely and it tends to get you paranoid.

So tripping in the past gets you schizophrenic, and tripping in the future tends to get you paranoid. Hang out in the here-and-now. It is healing. When you're in the here-and-now, accept it as reality. Don't think about it or run it through your mind-filter when it's coming in. Accept it.

—*This Season's People*, p. 30

Intellect

When one understands unsulliable nature of the intellect, it is no longer necessary to seek absolution for past sins. This is from the Tibetan tradition, as reported by W.Y. Evans-Wentz in *Tibetan Yoga* and *Secret Doctrines*.

I learned to understand this more fully when I was smoking some local grass that had come from a friend. I was surprised to find that it was very smart grass. Sometimes grass is sexy, sometimes it is sleepy, sometimes it is alert, sometimes it is artistic, and sometimes it is smart. This grass was smart.

I began to think about the unsulliable nature of the intellect and I thought, this is like the difference between hardware crazy and software crazy. If you are hardware crazy, you need to learn to work around it or seek medical help. If you are software crazy, the unsulliable nature of the intellect comes into play.

A computer has two kinds of memory. One kind is called ROM, or read-only memory. This means that it is a permanent, unchangeable set of instructions that tells the computer how to do normal operations like work the mouse or make type on the screen.

The other kind is called RAM, which stands for random-access memory. This is the actual working memory of the computer. It can take any form, such as a game or a check register or a word processor, that the software dictates.

New computer users are told that there is nothing you can say to a computer by way of the keyboard that will break or ruin it. If you manage to confuse it enough with conflicting instructions, then the most that can happen is it might lock up. In that case, you just restart it and all those mistakes are erased and the RAM comes back clean and perfect. This is the unsulliable nature of random-access memory.

You can't break or ruin your mind by anything you think. Your mind must be able to think anything. It must be able to consider all alternatives, no matter how awful or horrible. Your intellect is a perfect computer. If your mind couldn't consider all the alternatives, that would be something wrong in itself. It does not make you crazy to think a crazy thought. You can look at that crazy thought and say to yourself, "My, what a crazy thought," and go on about your life without having any fear that your mind has been damaged or dirtied in any lasting way by that passing nutty thought. This is the unsulliable nature of the intellect.

—*Cannabis Spirituality*, pp. 133-135

International Relations

People say, "How come China can get away with all this crap?"

Because they are an atomic nation, that's why. . .

And you can't say shit to an atomic nation.

You don't fight with an atomic nation. No matter how wrong-headed their trip is.

Kindness

People are supposed to take care of themselves and be kind and helpful to anybody who has problems. That has nothing to do with the government, or the law, or the Constitution, or anything like that.

Society should behave at the ethical best of its citizens, not at the lowest common denominator.

Laughter

Laughter? I think laughing's just free good karma. You know, all the time that you're laughing you're wide open, you're non-linear, non-directional. . . . It may be the highest form of communication that we can do by mouth.

—*Monday Night Class*

Lawyer Joke #1

In arguments, a lot of people say they want to take the part of the devil's advocate.

I don't know why they worry about the devil not having enough advocacy. . . hasn't he already got the lawyers?

Lawyer Joke #2

What do lawyers and sperm have in common?

They both have about one in a quarter-million chance of becoming a human being.

Marriage

I think you should be able to do a lifetime trip with somebody— and you can. You can get with somebody and say, "OK, if I'm not straight with you, I'm going to get straight with you." That's really important because, if you do a thing like that, when you do get straight, you know how come you got that way, and you're really tight, and you're on for the cruise. But both people have to want that to happen.

I was married a couple of times before, but I feel very settled now—I feel really lifetime, I just feel solid as a rock with this trip. It's the best thing I ever had going, and I really dig it.

The major thing about my earlier marriages was that we weren't in agreement on anything at all about getting straight, or being straight, or what straight was. What makes a marriage stay together is to want to be straight, and then put the energy to it— put it on the rock, man, and you can do it.

If you make it with a lifetime mate, you're really on for a good thing, because you can get more and more subtle, and heavier and heavier, and closer and closer, and more and more telepathic— and it's really lovely. It's a good thing to work out.

—"Monday Night Class, The New Edition" (unpublished)

Midwifery

In their work, the midwives have done many important things, but one of my favorites is proving the hippy energy assumptions in the objective arena of childbirth.

The midwives prove that vibes are real and that they make a difference. Their excellent statistics are the result, in large part, of their understanding of birth as a psychic event as well as a material event.

—*Cannabis Spirituality*, p. 67

• • •

The medical establishment has taken the mechanical part about as far as it can be sanely taken and maybe a little past that. The midwives have better numbers than the doctors from recognizing the spiritual dimension of childbirth.

The hospital closest to us in Tennessee has a 44 percent cesarean-section rate. A cesarean section means taking the baby out surgically through the belly, from a belief that the mother can't do it the normal way. Our midwives' cesarean-section rate is 1.7 percent.

—*Cannabis Spirituality*, pp. 67-68

Monday Night Class

It's funny.

I did some Monday night classes in Nashville, and because it was such a small meeting, my heckler had to cover being a necktie guy, a born-again Christian, and a drunk, all at once. He had to cover three bases, because we had so few people.

We started working and the owner comes out and says, "Let me throw this guy out."

And I said, "No! No! He is part of the action! It's part of what we've gotta do!"

—Television interview, THC (The Hemp Channel,
Seattle, WA), Vivian McPeak, host, 1999

Money

My Uncle Charlie, who has been a political activist—he helped organize the waterfront in San Francisco; he's always been on the side of the people—told me the story of the Golden Horns.

Once there was a kingdom so small that all of the citizens could fit in the king's courtyard. When there was an election, they called in all the citizens of the country to come and stand in the king's courtyard. The rich and the poor were all there, and it was said that this was a country with a fair system of government, because everyone could vote.

The King's vizier came out and read the resolution to be voted on. He read:

"Be it resolved, that the poor people shall pay all of the taxes, and the rich people shall pay none."

"All those in favor," he bellowed, "raise your golden horns and blow." And all the rich people raised their golden horns and blew a long, powerful note.

The King's vizier went on. "All those opposed," he said, "raise your golden horns and blow."

Not a sound was heard, for the poor people had no golden horns.

• • •

I've moved literally millions of dollars in my life and never have had any of it stick to me or tried to have any of it stick to me, because what I wanted to do was make the changes in those countries that needed the work.

• • •

One of my definitions of money is "fossilized laziness."

• • •

Today, we've got our values and priorities mixed up: One of my sons refers to basketball as "the tall men's charity."

• • •

There's no amount of money that would turn my head. I want to continue to be the same person I am and keep the same friends more than I want money.

• • •

I've always thought it was totally insane to give people Social Security and then tax some of it.

It doesn't seem unreasonable that if somebody paid into Social Security, they should benefit from it. But on the other hand, I think if you've become wealthy, you could say, "Throw my Social Security in the pot to help somebody who didn't make much money."

In Europe they have this concept of *noblesse oblige*. That's the idea that if you're favored by your circumstance, born into the nobility through no virtue of your own, that you owe something to the world. And you're supposed to use the power and privilege and education and money that you have at your disposal to try to do something to even it out for the whole world.

I mentioned that to a guy who was someone who did that. His name was Jacob Von Uxkull, and he had founded the Right Livelihood Award, of which I am one of the first winners. He was a Swedish nobleman who sold his stamp collection to start the Right Livelihood Award, and he's been giving $25,000 and $30,000 cash awards away, five and six a year, since 1980.

So I was talking to him and I said, "Well, the trouble in America is that we don't have any *noblesse oblige*."

And he said, "Well, you don't have any nobles."

And I said, "Yeah. . . and they ain't obliged to do something either."

• • •

There used to be the concept of a "dollar-a-year man." That's some rich guy who would go put in a term working at some job for the government, and only take a dollar a year, saying, "I'm coming in here to help sort it out; I am not coming in to make money on it."

• • •

A dude who is hereditarily rich and has the stuff to care about other people when he's already got it knocked is just a noble thing.

NAFTA and GATT

The thing about NAFTA and GATT is that the corporations can knock down local laws if they consider them to be in restraint of any kind of free trade they want to be doing. It's like if this gas company comes into Canada with some stuff in it that's a known cancer-causer or pollutant, and it's against the law to do it in Canada, and Canada stops this gas company at the border, and the gas company sues Canada in Canada's own supreme court and beats them under the terms of NAFTA and GATT and makes them have to take this stuff with this cancer-causer in it.

That's what [the North American Free Trade Agreement and the General Agreement on Tariffs and Trade] are about.

—Television interview, THC (The Hemp Channel,
Seattle, WA), Vivian McPeak, host, 1999

Nonviolence

What if somebody came in and was going to take over your country and not let you practice your religion and arrest you for doing it? My friend Peter was asked that by the Lions Club one time and had to remind them that someone had already come into our country (the Farm) and wouldn't let us practice our religion, and weren't they glad that we were nonviolent?

But that question is very unfair. There's nobody in the continental United States, or in any territory that we really have any right to, who is doing anything like that. But we, on the other hand, are doing that to scores of other countries around the world.

So the question is not what we're going to do if someone comes to get us; it's more of what we're doing to other people.

The United States is not in any immediate danger. Other people are in danger from us.

By being nonviolent, we're trying to reduce the probability of its happening. We're being actively nonviolent. We're like anti-terrorists. In order to keep Latin America from invading the United States, we're trying to help out south of the border. And in order to help keep Africa from jumping off on the United States, well-deserved though it might be, we're over in Lesotho doing something about it. If you're a pacifist, you act ahead of time, before the violence starts. If you're not a pacifist, you act when the violence starts.

—*Rendered Infamous*

• • •

When you read the histories of the discovery and conquest of Mexico and Peru, by Cortez and Pizarro, it doesn't really make it plain what a high level of civilization was destroyed by the *conquistadores*. Some of the cities of the Maya, which were destroyed, were older and bigger than the cities in Europe where those *conquistadores* had come from. Their calendar was more accurate.

The web of citizenry and ecology in Peru, for instance, was so highly evolved that, in that mountainous land, there was a level of crops and a kind of corn for every altitude change from the coast to the 20,000-foot peaks by Machu Picchu. There was a kind of corn that grew at every altitude, and there was commerce all the way from those peaks down to the ocean.

The way the society was designed was beautiful, elegant in its efficiency. There were people who always lived at the beach. There were people who always lived in the foothills. There were people who always lived in the low mountains, and there were people who always lived in the high mountains. The people who lived in an area would carry goods across their own territory, to which they had become adapted over ages of time. When they got to the edge of the foothills, the beach people would set [the goods] down, and the low-altitude ones would pick them up and carry them up to the middle altitudes, across their own territory. They would then set them down and they would [be taken] across the next territory by people who lived in the middle altitudes all the time, and were adapted to it.

It took thousands of years to develop a system with a kind of corn for every level of altitude, and a kind of people for every level of altitude. When the Spanish came in and conquered that country, it was not a military feat, but merely the destruction of that beautiful system, which worked better than the one that is there now.

These are gross examples of the breakdown of systems all over the world. Western civilization is an entropy maker, a trash producer, an inflation generator, a war profiteer, and a misery maker. People who defend it are ignorant, because they do not understand what it has done to the world.

It is kinder to starve because the weather was bad than to starve because somebody made a mistake, or somebody was greedy and took your livelihood away. Grief is easier to bear when it comes from God than when it comes from man. Man is very arrogant to make his grief and his affliction be heavier on mankind than the affliction that God had already allotted for mankind.

—*Rendered Infamous*, pp. 94-95

• • •

Our society works to convey the notion that a conscientious objector is not a patriot.

When I was 10 years old, I was at Camp Hale, Colorado, where Bob Dole was. It was the Army cold-weather training base. It was also a camp for German prisoners of war, and it was also a camp for conscientious objectors—and the conscientious objectors were kept in the same section and in the same conditions with the prisoners of war.

In World War I, they used to shoot conscientious objectors.

Oneness

I know something. I know we're all One. I know it so well that if I'm falling out of a tree, I know we're all One before I hit the ground. I'm not going to forget it; I can't give it up.

—*This Season's People*, p. 24

Perfect

The way you make yourself better is to assume that you are perfect, because each one of us is perfect. . . the doctrine of perfection says: If I draw a circle, it may not be a perfect circle, but it's a perfect whatever it is. Yay. That's really true, because that's what each one of us is—a perfect whatever we are. And we're all perfect. Assuming that you're perfect means assuming that you can change, and that you can become however you ought to be.

—*Monday Night Class*

Prison

A friend of mine once said in the penitentiary:

> Stone walls and steel bars do not a prison make. But you
> throw in some bad food and bad mattresses, obnoxious
> guards and a general lack of amenities, and you've got
> something.

—*Rendered Infamous*, p. 16

• • •

The people in the penitentiary who were sad were not the strong,
amusing people like W.T. Hardison or the long-timers; my heart
wept for the ones they called the "punks." Not what you'd call a
punk on the street. Not some tough kid in a leather jacket backing
off humanity with the snarl and screech from an electric guitar.
The punks were 18-year-olds and occasional 17-year-olds that
some jury out in the country somewhere had seen fit to send to the
penitentiary. They could be seen walking around the exercise yard
with shaved heads when all the other prisoners had long hair.
They wore ill-fitting clothes and crept around in the corners, trying to stay away from people. Because of their youth, because they
were not fully grown and did not have a man's musculature to defend themselves with, they were sometimes the repeated victims
of prison homosexual rape.

I was once thrown into a cell with three young men. One was
quiet and nondescript, and I can't remember him very well, because the other two were so stunning in their character types. One
was about 22, strong and well-built, six feet, maybe 175 pounds,
with bright red hair, sunbleached yellow-blond eyebrows, and a
ruddy complexion—a handsome, beautiful young man in his
prime. The other, with his shaved head and his saggy-bottomed
pants, had been pushed as a punk so long that he had begun to
play the role. The young man was so driven by his hormones that
his eyes grew red like a bull. The shaved-headed boy rolled his
t-shirt up in a simulacrum of a brassiere and belly-danced while I
sat in the corner and read comic books. Not what you would call
"gay," but just pure prison lust.

I heard the red-haired boy say, "You just hammer them up alongside the head enough times and that old jaw opens."

The convicts say, If you can't do the time, then don't do the crime. Of all the possible failings catalogued in the penitentiary, the worst is to fall weak.

The reason I'm coming out of the penitentiary talking this way is not because I was damaged so much by it, because I, after all, am supposed to be a professional keep-it-together person. They would have been able to laugh and hoot and point quite a lot if I had rolled over and folded up in their old penitentiary, so I wasn't about to. But I had a lot going for me. I got to read spiritual books, and I got a lot of support. My family was not down on me and didn't hate me because of what I'd done. Nobody felt like I'd betrayed them. I didn't have any bad vibes coming from the Farm because of what I'd done. It was actually a burn for me to have to do the time since I'd been against planting [the pot] anyway, so I had optimum conditions going into it. So I'm not saying all this horrendous stuff in the nature of a complaint. But if a young person, 18 years old, maybe, does something crazy, maybe drunk, maybe barely knows what he's doing, he can find himself slapped into a place that is outside the United States and as away from the protection of the Constitution as if it were on another planet.

The insides of penitentiaries do not belong to the world; they belong to hell. They have different ground rules. There is no order inside the penitentiary. There is a minimum of order imposed on it, and a maximum of infrastructure to keep order: cells and bars and special lights and electric eyes and guns and mace and uniformed guards and radio and all of that to create order, and there isn't any order. Standing in line and eating at the same time is not order.

The life that goes on—not for the people like me who just came in for a year, but for the people who are going to be there a long time and have to put together some kind of a life to live inside that place—is something else.

I'm reminded of one guy I saw complaining to Sergeant Fury one time about a problem he had. The next time I saw him, several days later, he came walking by and he had on a prison shirt, sleeves torn off, and a picture of a beautiful, long-haired hippy boy on his back, with a very light, downy mustache and little bits of golden curls along his cheekbones, and long hair—a beautiful hippy boy. And he said to Sergeant Fury, "You know that problem I was telling you about that I had? I ain't got no problem anymore. Everything's all right now."

What he was alluding to was that, through bribery or political power or some means or other, he had arranged to have someone transferred into his cell whom he could intimidate into being his submissive lover. So he didn't have a problem anymore, because he had managed to get somebody in his cell he could handle. He was going to live there for the rest of his life and who was going to be in that cell with him was his wife, whether or not they had had some other life before that.

I'm not talking about the day trippers. It hurts them, and it damages their life. But for the people you just stick in there, 50, 60, 70 years is meaningless.

When they're fixing to let you out, they tell you, "Hey, you're getting out today! It's time to pack your junk and kiss your punk."

"Drop your cocks and get your box."

A "shiv" used to be prison talk for a knife. But shiv isn't prison talk for a knife anymore—it's old-fashioned. Prison talk for a knife is now a "shank." I don't know whether that's the shank of a spoon, or like the steel shank out of a shoe, but somehow, it's shank. They used to say that the prison love song was, Shit on my dick or blood on my shank. I know this is a little rough for public consumption, but I wanted you to know what you were doing when you send young people to the penitentiary, where you are sending them, and what you are exposing them to. What did you think you would get back after exposing them to that?

—*Rendered Infamous*, pp. 150-153

Religion

Well, the thing about all. . . religions is that you can stack them all up together like IBM cards, and you can look at them and see which holes go all the way through. And that's the trip we're trying to do, the one with the holes that go all the way through.

—*The Caravan*

Republicans

We're not trying to outlaw Republicans. We're not trying to get rid of them or anything like that. We're just saying that their kind of games should not affect anybody else's health, livelihood, diet, chances for education, or anything like that. If they want to go into the arena and play gladiator hard-ball with money, that's fine. . . but the people in the stands are not supposed to suffer in any way from it.

• • •

The Republicans do not say "the Democratic Party." They do not say that; they never use that phrase. They say "the Democrat Party." You just listen, and pay attention, and watch what those guys say. . . and they don't say "Democratic." They go to circumlocution to avoid saying that.

Responsibility

A person can do wonders on their efforts—aided and unaided—and has obligations to play fair. . . and the stronger and smarter you are, the more your obligation is to play fair.

• • •

The myth of the free market assumes some parity among the horse-traders. In olden times, there were proscriptions against usury that were in effect from the Church, when usury was against the law. Not only usury, but there was a level short of usury which was considered, if not a legal matter, at least an ecclesiastical matter, and people would be warned against the un-Christian nature of "sharp practices." Sharp practices included the kind of farming mentality that confused husbandry with being sure to plant the fruit trees on the side of the property close to the fence, so the shade would fall on your neighbor's property and the fruit would fall on your own. At that level, there are many things that could be done by a farmer that could be considered "sharp practices." But the Bible taught that the first two rows along the edge of the road were dedicated to passing travelers who, in those days of non-frozen or perishable foods, could not possibly carry enough food for a very long journey, and probably didn't have any actual money on their persons as they traveled. These were cultural norms. Some may say that is naive and it was easier then, and there are more people now and times are harder. But two rows alongside the field of a giant, complicated farm are virtually insignificant.

There are huge quantities of food produced and harvested these days, but two rows could still be done without damage to the industry. It is merely that sharp practices have become "normal," which is to say not right or acceptable, but done by so many people that the curve describing the frequency of that action is near the norm.

—Rendered Infamous

Rich, Poor, and Balance of Power

The balance of rich to poor is getting worse all the time.

It's just a fact of sociology that the more of an imbalance there is between rich and poor, the heavier the nature of the police force that it takes to enforce it. Because it is enforced. It is not voluntary, it's not liked, it's not appreciated. . . it is enforced.

And when it gets to the deal where the guys who are doing the enforcing have the license to put 41 bullets in a guy because he's the wrong color and scares 'em. . . the enforcement has gone insane.

Right Livelihood Award Reunion

I have just returned from a week-long trip to Salzburg, Austria, where I was attending the 20th anniversary reunion of the winners of the Right Livelihood Award, or—as it is known in Europe—The Alternative Nobel Prize.

Salzburg is as fancy as Disneyland, as well as being made of stone, and in good taste. We had cocktails with the Governor in a thousand-year-old castle. I noticed that the steps were kind of strange. The risers were only about four inches high, and the treads were about two and a half feet broad. One of the nuns, Sister Rosalie, was up on history and told us that they were that way because they were horse stairs. She said, "You didn't think kings were going to walk upstairs, did you?"

The Right Livelihood Award was founded in 1980 by Jacob Von Uxkull, a young Swedish nobleman. He felt that it cheapened the Nobel Prize when the award went to the likes of Henry Kissinger and other politicians. What Jacob meant by right livelihood was that the way that one made one's living did not damage the environment or other people's livelihood and helped out overall.

I have the honor of being the first winner of this award, along with Hassan Fathey, an Egyptian architect. My award was for founding our community, the Farm, in Summertown, Tennessee, in 1971, and for founding our overseas relief and development company, called Plenty International, in 1974. I donated my $25,000 cash award to Plenty for further project work.

I missed the 10th anniversary meeting so this was my first chance to see the other winners. By now this group has grown to over 70 members. I couldn't possibly mention all of them, but I will say that they were from 44 countries. There were two nuns, one in social service in Trinidad, the other an expert on nuclear and transnuclear weapons.

There was a bishop and several MDs. One of the doctors had used his influence to create 180 paramedics who cover a whole district of Bangladesh and to start a generic drug company for cheaper prescriptions. There was a woman who was an Israeli lawyer who spent two decades defending Palestinians in Israeli courts.

A woman from India had helped Indian villages declare themselves "Monsanto-free areas" and helped them keep their seeds instead of buying the ones with the sterile second generation.

One of my favorites was Hans-Peter Durr, who had been the Director of the Max Planck Institute for 15 years. He knew such illustrious physicists as Edward Teller and Werner Heisenberg. He got his award for pointing out that there was no physics to support Ronald Reagan's "Star Wars" plan. He was undeniably one of the most brilliant men in the world and he was sweet and down-home and fun to talk to—altogether the way we would like smart people to be.

They are all very afraid of what they call globalization, which, among other things, allows transnational corporations to go into small countries and compete with local business. People in the small countries are not trying to be Americans and failing at it. They like being what they are. They aspire to good medicine and sanitation, as we all do, but they don't want to have to quit being who they are to participate in it.

I was chatting with one of the other winners, Patrick van Rensburg, a white South African diplomat who resigned in protest of apartheid and worked to end it. We were noticing the high level of accomplishment and intelligence in the people Jacob had assembled and Patrick said, in a fair Tennessee accent, "Well, you know that there are 7,422 guitar pickers in Nashville." And I remembered the next line, "And every one of them pick better than I will."

One thing that tended to break my heart a little was the way so many of the people from the small countries were fearful of and angry at the U.S. foreign and financial policies. I am old enough to remember when we liberated Europe and the people ran out in the street to hug and kiss our troops. I miss that.

Conspiracy theories abounded. Sometimes I tried to help out. I told them that "Not even in Washington, DC, are they stupid enough to hit the Chinese Embassy on purpose." I also told them that the ordinary people of America were not out to get them. They were very sweet. Some of them said that they hoped that I didn't feel bad to hear the U.S. criticized. I admitted that we weren't very self-critical at all and it was kind of refreshing to hear some.

Rock 'n' Roll

The hippies did massive things. . . among them, rock 'n' roll.

Rock 'n' roll was a shadow before the hippies picked it up. Then it became the music of the entire world for decades. It became political, revolutionary.

Hippies made rock 'n' roll the international language of young people.

When I go out in my white beard and ponytail, young street boys on the streets in Guatemala and places like that do two gestures: toking and picking.

• • •

Little Richard I have an affinity for, but Elvis Presley looked like the ones who used to beat me up.

He didn't have an ounce of politics in him. He used the black people's stuff and just peeled it right off. He was popularizing stuff that was done by other people. He had a smooth face like a baby's bottom, and I don't want to get into the middle of thinking about Elvis being the King or not. But when the time capsule hits out there in Alpha Centauri, and they look and see what's in the time capsule, they're going to say, "Send more Chuck Berry."

• • •

Chuck Berry, Fats Domino, Little Richard. . . what they were trying to do was just be able to get into the back doors of the clubs. They were breaking trail in the race world.

Early black rockers and jazz guys were playing in places where they wouldn't even let them eat.

That's what they were fighting for.

• • •

The early rockers were talking girls, they weren't talking revolution. They were living revolution by taking their music out into white clubs. They were living it by what they were doing, but they weren't singing it.

• • •

I noticed that one of my sons was not impressed with Jimmy Hendrix's *Star Spangled Banner*, and I questioned him about it for a while. . . until I realized that he didn't know the words.

You gotta hear Hendrix's version and know the words. When he's playing crash boom and all that stuff on the guitar, the words going on behind it are "The bombs bursting in air." It's a very ironical piece of music, because it's about a tortured country that's not living up to its ideals.

Hendrix's version of the *Star Spangled Banner* is still the one I cry for.

• • •

I don't like vile lyrics in rock 'n' roll. I may be a medium-dirty-talking hippy—but I allow for people's mothers and stuff.

Self-Discipline

If you're not steering your mind, it's running on automatic pilot and goes a million times faster than you can steer it.

—*This Season's People,* p. 42

Sex and Sex Education

A sexually not permissive, but warm and friendly society has got to be more healthy than a Puritanical, uptight one.

• • •

The same people who don't want you to have abortions also don't want you to have sex education in schools.

The lack of sex education sticks the kids out to the mercy of their hormones with no instructions.

• • •

The result of trying to regulate sex is that the sexually disenfranchised can't find a way to have normal human relaxation that everybody in the world gets to have but them. So the guys who rub up against you in the elevators, and stuff like that, don't really want somebody's little girl or a movie star. If some lady of their own age who was maybe not even that foxy-looking, but kind and generous, would give some, they would probably be really improved by that.

With sexual stuff, the worse you repress it, the more "cathexis" or psychological power it gets behind it, and the more you repress it, the harder it is to deal with.

You ought to be able to go down to a little movie in Times Square and whack off by yourself, as long as you dispose of your Kleenex neatly.

• • •

You can't cut off the sex life of the world. The more you try, the crazier it gets. And the crazier it gets, the more people you have driven to kidnapping a child, driven to killing a child because of what will happen to them for kidnapping it.

• • •

If kids, instead of being told that "Sex is only for when you're married to have babies," were told that heavy petting is quite a lot of fun and it does not make you pregnant. . . if they had a little education about stuff like that, they could experiment and play around the edges of love without getting pregnant on the first try.

And there are ways we could let children discover their sexual feelings without having to make love.

There's the old concept of "bundling," for instance. It's the old Puritan thing of when people were courting, with the permission of the parents, they could go to bed clothed in the cold weather—when it was hard to keep anything warm—and they could hang out together in bed and cuddle and smooch clothed.

And it was called "bundling."

And it was a lovely old winter-time sport.

So even the most grim, Puritanical people in the world still get those sexual feelings when just courting.

• • •

One of the problems with sex education is that trying to tell people how to do sex is already clinical as soon as you open your mouth.

What you can say is that you can have a humorous attitude, and you can have a kindly attitude, but you cannot freak out over things.

People freak out because little boys play with themselves. Well, when it's right there at the end of your arm's reach, what do you expect?

• • •

I was told one time by a European boy that he noticed that people in America don't learn about sex well, because he noticed that all of the boys he sees in the gym obviously always whack off with the same hand, because they always point in the same direction—away from the dominant hand. "And in Europe," he said, "we were taught to change hands, so you wouldn't hang one way or another."

Now there's a level of technique!

• • •

Most of the stuff in the *Kama Sutra* could be invented by two honest 18-year-olds on a rainy Saturday afternoon.

• • •

We have so many conflicting messages in our country about sex. On the one hand, we have attitudes that are almost as bad as the Arabs about letting any female stuff show publicly. . . and then we have these bathing suits that are cut so high that there's almost no point in wearing anything.

• • •

I'm interested in running a healthy society. It's not so much that I'm a leftist or rightist as it is that I am sure that there are certain agreements with the biological realities of who we are.

I'm more for kindness.

If that's expressed in the way we do these things, we wouldn't have people who are so desperately horny that they go and do something cruel and stupid and inhumane about it. The word "desperate" comes from the Spanish *desperado*, which means "one without hope."

Spirituality

I feel that it's not so much techniques as it is [to] straighten up. Buddha says, "Avoid error." How about that?

—*The Caravan*

Suing

I think that one of the stupidest things that's being talked about these days is the idea that you get to sue for some money that you might have made. I thought in capitalism you took your chances, and if the cheetah chews your leg off, then you're a one-legged dude.

Technology

I think we can appreciate a minimal level of sane technology. But I cannot find it in myself to appreciate General Motors, or Westinghouse, or General Atomics as consumer-feeding entities. I think that worship of technology is a mistake, actually.

Like medical care, technology should be introduced on the basis of what we need rather than what we can be sold. I must admit that I love my Macintosh and I am an e-mail user. I am even going to get one of those new little satellite dishes. But I drive a 27-year-old Volvo that I maintain myself, and I like it better than this year's model.

I think technology is an ingrown speed trip that humankind got hooked on. If you step out for a while and take a look at a city from a distance and dig it for a few days, you can find out what it is that you really do need and don't need.

—"Monday Night Class, The New Edition" (unpublished)

Tobacco

Kids down in Tennessee are chewing tobacco. And kids in the grade schools have what they call "Skol holes," which are ulcers in the gums from Skol snuff. They do this in the classrooms.

—Unpublished interview for *Free Spirit* magazine, with Paul English, William Meyers, Stephany Evans, and Marc Greene, 1995

Unwanted Pregnancy

On the Farm, we used to teach a lovely form of birth control that did not require condoms. All it required was friendly cooperation between people.

Wasn't that good for one-night stands, I suppose.

We discovered that there were two or three ways within a woman's power that she could pinpoint exactly when she ovulated. . . not down to like a week or something, but down to the hour.

Knowing that, you could just avoid that time. . . and then be free the rest of the time.

• • •

When they say that a girl is liable to get pregnant if she has a low self-concept, what they mean by a low self-concept, really, is that not enough people love her.

Values

You must have a personal code. There must be moral imperatives in your life. There must be things that you don't stoop to do and things that you are obliged to do. Having a personal code is like having a set of instruments to fly by in the dark or in a storm like an airplane. When an airplane is flying by instruments, there are dials and gauges on the instrument panel that tell the pilot if the plane is tilted to one side or the other and if altitude is being gained or lost and which way the plane is going. If it is dark or cloudy, the pilot has to fly by the information in the plane. In one's personal life, principles are the instruments that can be used to steer by when it is crazy out.

—*Cannabis Spirituality*, p. 129

Humanity

[During my year in prison] there was another prisoner there called Madame Razor Blade, who was supposed to have done something unspeakable to his family—dismembered them, perhaps, and left them in the trunk of a car. He dressed as close to a woman as he could, within the limits of the penitentiary garb, and he had his act down pretty good. He wore a bright pink washcloth tucked in his collar like a scarf, and he wore his pants pulled as high as he could pull them, and belted his belt as tight as he could, until it made a little waist, and an imitation of the round bottom of a woman. He had his moves down pretty cold. He moved like a woman. He combed his hair in a hairdo that was a pretty good imitation of a standard Tennessee lady's beehive, bubble-hair hairdo.

When you caught Razor Blade out of the corner of your eye, and saw his moves, it made you snap your neck and say, "What? Is there a woman here in the joint?"

And then you got your head turned and saw what it was you snapped for. Razor Blade would be there, and he would smile and look at you with that look that said, just as clear as anything, "Got you again, didn't I?"

Even at that, the other prisoners in the pen didn't like to see the guards bust into Razor Blade's cell and take away all his pretty stuff. They thought it was wrong to take away from Razor Blade whatever little it was that he had.

I watched Razor Blade from a distance until one day, standing in the chow line, picking up a cup of fruit juice out of the cooler, I found myself face to face with Madame Razor Blade, who looked at me, and the telepathy was as clear as a bell.

Without ever opening his mouth, just from eye to eye, he said, You say you love people. You say that everybody's worth something. You say you believe in being kind. Are you going to recognize me as a human being? Are you going to look in my eyes and say hello to me as a human being? Or are you going to turn your back on me because of what I did?

I could not turn my back on him. I had to look him in the eye and acknowledge his presence in the world and say, "Howdy," which is to say, "How do ye?" and recognize his humanity.

Something changed in me then, and I knew I could not be exactly the same way I was, even about someone who had taken a life.

—*Rendered Infamous*, pp. 145-146

Violence

I understood that some people took this Marine business very seriously. Much more seriously than I did, I could tell right away.

All the physical training, all the bayonet training, all the judo training, all the obstacle courses, did me no good whatsoever. I went back to Santa Fe on my boot leave and ran into the same bully who had beaten me up five times all the way through high school. He took one look at my Marine Corps uniform and proceeded to beat me up again, just to show me where it was really at.

Welfare

What we have now is capitalism for poor people and welfare for rich people.

• • •

Ideally, we're all supposed to live at a level several times better than what the government guarantees.

• • •

It isn't just losing an arm or a leg or being blind or something that makes it difficult for somebody to make it. There are folks that have handicaps like that who just completely rise above them and have whole lives that don't have anything to do with winning foot races.

But at the same time, there're other folks who look like they've got all their stuff, and what they haven't got is the confidence to talk to anybody much. . . or maybe they're just not real swift and can do something if someone could keep them lined out on it but wouldn't go and start a business on their own, or anything. And they're folks who just need some help.

And they shouldn't have to live in squalor, and they shouldn't have to live without health care—and all of that—because of that.

The way it is, though, is that the society has become so individualistic and so stingy that it is quite unpleasant.

• • •

They keep talking about welfare ripping off the public, and that's such a shame. The worst of the welfare people just take a drop in the bucket. The people who rip off welfare and the people who rip off Medicaid are the doctors, and clinics, and hospitals, and HMOs. They're the ones who do the big, million-dollar rip-offs.

Some welfare mother, by staying on welfare another year, would account for only probably 3 to 4 days in a hospital that some HMO would rip people off of.

• • •

The thing about this recent story of the little 6-year-old who shot the girl at school is that the reason he was staying at that nasty place he was staying, where they had guns lying around on the floor, is that his mother had gotten kicked off welfare and was working two jobs. This guy her son was staying with was the only relation of hers that she could leave her kid with.

That's what happens to people when they get off welfare and the press or government boasts, "Oh, we cut the welfare rolls by 20 percent". . . and they don't tell you about those people who got cut off of it.

I don't think the government should quibble about child care if you have an 18-year-old mother and she's willing to work and go to school. I think the government should give her A-number-1,

U.S. government–inspected, grade A health care and child care. . . and that kid should be as safe as possible.

A mother should not have to leave her kid with some half-assed cousin who has guns in the house. . . which this woman was driven to do by the stinginess of the welfare system.

She was forced to do it because this is not a good job market on the bottom end. In fact, it's kind of amazing that we're so blatant about it that someone like Greenspan says, "Well, the market's getting so good that it's getting so that poor people are going to have to get paid more for doing the shit-work, and we're going to have to cool the market."

And the people he thinks are doing so well who are doing the shit-work say, "Oh! I thought I was just gonna be able to like maybe have my own apartment!"

• • •

They come down on these girls who get pregnant and leave their babies someplace. The only thing on the district attorney's mind in those cases is whether he can get first-degree murder or is he gonna have to settle for second?

They expect some 15-year-old, knocked-up girl having her baby alone by herself to be perfectly smart and make no bad decisions for herself in a situation that doctors in hospitals tell grown-up ladies that they have to be drugged to the teeth just to withstand.

That's part of the overall cruelty of the country that I see as really wrong.

• • •

Why do we need an uneducated, unvaccinated, diseased lower class running around to hold up our liquor stores for us?

It's like the old Greek story of sowing dragon's teeth—where you sow dragon's teeth and armed soldiers grow up out of the ground.

We're sowing dragon's teeth: We're building the social ills of the future.

This is so Republican.

It's the same thing we did to Russia. Gorbachev takes the leap of faith, and then we stiff 'em and don't help 'em convert, and we allow the Russian mafia to take over and eat up what little bit of aid they get, and we don't help them become a market economy. We just cut them loose and say, "Nanny, boo-boo. . . we got you guys."

That was really stupid.

• • •

The way we've got to correct the welfare situation is reminiscent of what happened to us in Guatemala. When we were in Guatemala, people were bringing us dying babies, and we said, "We've got to get back upstream from this. We've got to start feeding those pregnant women."

In the same way, we've got to go back upstream and get things coming down better. We've got to start interceding in this welfare situation earlier than we do.

Now, what usually happens is that we have a really lower-class person going through a divorce, say, and the judge applies some formula of compensation that the guy is just going to never be able to do—imposes a middle-class alimony on him and the poor guy never made that much money in his life.

That's just a double-bind, and in psychology they say that it's the double-bind that will drive you crazy.

We've got to not only teach people to be responsible, we have to make sure that they're able to get jobs where they can do something to get out from under their poverty.

• • •

When you have a culture where you're taught to be mean, where the law wants to be mean. . . people on the street are calling for capital punishment.

• • •

The thing about the best of the United States and the best about the Farm, and the thing that people in the United States don't understand about Cuba, is what it's like to be in it all together.

We're not in it all together, here. Some of us are in it one way and some of us are in it another way.

We're in the largest peacetime financial expansion in history and still have a bunch of real poor people.

That means that those people have no reason to participate in our society.

We've got to recognize that we're all a portion of the earth. We're here together in this community, in this town, in this house, in this neighborhood, in this country, on this planet.

We're all here together, and here's where it is right now.

Words

. . . words are very, very heavy magic. So everything you say is true. You only think you can lie, but you can't really. The secret words of the masters are: "I Am." You must be very careful what you say next.

—*Monday Night Class*

WTO

Hitler was so obviously evil. Comic books could tell that he was evil. But you've gotta get into a little bit more about the WTO to see what's really wrong with it: The wolf in sheep's clothing is a lot more frightening because it looks like a sheep.

• • •

The World Trade Organization is actually taking the sovereignty of countries without firing a shot.

Awesome!

PART III

And in
Conclusion

CHAPTER 21

The Last Word

I'm a general semanticist who believes it's never possible to say all there is to say about anything, and that any time you say something, at the end you should say "Etc."—because you haven't said all there is to say about anything.

Etc.

A Personal Letter

Hi there to all my friends and supporters, and those learning about me for the first time who think, hey, there might be some pretty good stuff here.

First of all, I'm so grateful you folks are out there wanting to do good things, and I'm looking forward to hearing from more of you as I go along.

One idea I have is to put people in touch with each other who are interested in my campaign so you all can talk back and forth to each other, find out what resources you all have and can share, and generally have a little pre-election electronic party going on. Let me know if it's OK to attach your e-mail address to my outgoing messages to supporters so they can contact you. You'll get those same messages, so you'll have other people's addresses too. Also let me know if it's OK to quote some of your glowing statements on my behalf.

I'm really interested in expanding the Green Party during this campaign, so I want to urge you to organize in your local area, find out who your Greens are, get others to register Green, and let them know that I sent you. Here are some of the things you can do to help:

1. Hunt up the Greens in your state and ask them how to register with the Green Party in your state. Don't forget to tell them I sent you. You can start by going to the Web site, http://www.greens.org/. This will take you directly to a screen that allows you to select your state and find out who your contacts are. It also gives you background information on the party, platform, history, and more.

   If there is no Green Party in your state, you may not be able to vote in the primary, but you can vote for anybody you want in the general election.

2. Print out copies of this and other info about the campaign from the Web for friends who don't have Internet access.

3. Pass on this information to everyone you think might be interested. Talk up the important issues and keep the energy high with the people around you who share the vision.

4. Some of my books are available from me by e-mail at stephen7@usit.net. Be sure to put BOOK ORDER in the subject line. They are $10 each. If you like, you can add $1, $2, or more to the purchase price of your book(s) to be contributed to the campaign. Now available are:

Rendered Infamous. Although written some time ago, this book outlines my position on the State in many ways.

Cannabis Spirituality. This contains much of the rationale for my political moves.

This Season's People. A philosophical book of essays you can carry in your pocket.

5. Although we won't need nearly the amount of money that the Republicrats are going to waste, we have a few things we'd like to do, like fly out to a venue that couldn't afford to pay for me, produce campaign literature, and pay the folks in the trenches. Donations up to $100 need no formality; if you want to give more than that, talk to me by e-mail.

    This is a poor people's campaign not just by accident, but because we want the real input from the people who are left out by the World Trade Organization.

6. Let us know if you'd like to put in some time, what area of expertise you have, and when you are available. We won't turn down any help we can get. Let us know where you are, and if you want to bring me to your area. I would prefer to stay with local contacts rather than in hotels or motels.

    We'll be putting up a wish list soon, and would love to have some creative donations. With your help, we think this can be a pretty fun campaign.

http://www.Stephen2000.org

Bio

I was born in Denver, Colorado, in 1935. I served three years in the Marine Corps during the Korean War, where I saw combat for several months. I received my B.A. degree (cum laude) in English and creative writing in 1962, and my M.A. in language arts in 1964, both from San Francisco State College (now University). After serving as an instructor in creative writing and general semantics for two years at San Francisco State (1964–1966), I began what came to be known as Monday Night Class. This weekly meeting started with six people and within three years was drawing 1500 mostly young people to participate in discussions about politics, religion, psychedelic drugs, sex, and the Vietnam War.

In 1970, I spoke at a San Francisco conference attended by preachers from throughout the country. They persuaded me to organize a speaking tour later that year of 42 of their towns and cities. I made the several-month tour with my family in a school bus camper, accompanied by about 300 Monday Night Class participants who petitioned to come along in 60 campers. The Caravan, as it was called, became the largest counterculture community in the nation before parking in the spring of 1971 in rural Tennessee, where Caravaners pooled their money to buy a 1750-acre tract of hilly, wooded land.

The Farm, as it came to be called, turned out to be the fastest-growing intentional community of the 1960s and 1970s, rising to 1300 people by 1977. All Farm members agreed to eschew alcohol, tobacco, animal products, and welfare. The newcomers to Tennessee grew their own food and created their own housing, water system, midwifery service, primary health care system, paramedic and ambulance service, and telephone systems. The Farm is internationally famous for at least three major accomplishments:

- that it survives nearly three decades after its founding,

- that it popularized tofu and soy milk as the basis of delicious vegetarian cuisine, and

- that its midwifery service published its excellent maternal and infant outcomes, accomplishing these results with extremely low rates of cesarean section and other obstetrical interventions.

In 1974, I founded and served as first Chairman of the Board of Directors of Plenty International, an international relief and development organization that, among other projects, helped rebuild 1200 houses, many schools, and installed water pipes to many village neighborhoods after the devastating Guatemala earthquake of 1976. Other projects were carried out in Lesotho, Belize, and southern Mexico. Plenty projects in the United States included the Jefferson Award–winning South Bronx Ambulance service in New York City, which cut the ambulance response time from 45 minutes to 7 minutes.

In 1974, three other Farm members and I served one- to three-year sentences in the Tennessee State Penitentiary as a result of some members having planted marijuana shortly after settling on the land. My book *Rendered Infamous* recounts this period of my life. A class action suit on my behalf returned voting rights to more than a quarter of a million convicts.

I was the 1980 winner of the first Right Livelihood Award from the Right Livelihood Foundation (Europe's Alternative Nobel Prize).

I've authored 11 books and currently serve as General Manager and Production Director of *Birth Gazette*, a midwifery quarterly. I've founded Rocinante, a community project for aging activists that combines with a birth center and midwifery service.

We're the only country among the industrialized, so-called civilized countries of the world that doesn't have socialized medicine. Well, of course, it should be single-payer, it should come from the government. We're the country where Hospital Corporation of America is going around to other countries and buying hospitals that are not for profit and taking them into profit. We're trying to stop the rest of the world from having health care. But in actuality, the rest of the world takes care of all of its citizens.

When I was up in Canada one time, I was talking about doctors, and this guy said, "Boy, you talk about your doctors bad. How come you talk about your doctors so bad?"

I said, "Don't you talk about your doctors like that?"

He said, "No, our doctors take care of us."

Then someone else said, "Yeah. . . everybody has health care here."

It blew my mind, 'cause I had been habitually pissed at doctors for a long time, and these guys did not feel like that.

That was some years ago. They might feel differently now, though, since the Americans have been hammering away on their system as hard as they can, 'cause it makes the Americans look so rotten to have them next door, doing it so well and everybody liking it.

• • •

That idea that there's something wrong with socialized medicine. . . that's some kind of old anti-Commie bugaboo.

I ain't no Commie.

"Socialized" means that it's done for the sake of society.

• • •

Since we give these corporations absolute hunting and fishing rights on the population to rip us off in every way they can devise, shouldn't we at least be allowed to be healthy while we're being ripped off?

• • •

I'm not advocating socialized medicine just for the poor but for everyone. Everyone gets the same kind, the same quality, of medical care that the congressmen and the President now get.

• • •

Whenever I look at something, I look at it with a public health attitude. . . and that goes for everything from some kinds of drugs being legalized and others not.

• • •

What we want is not-for-profit national health care.

• • •

We all pay for public health care, and we get it cheaper than letting the doctors run it on their own, without the government being in on it—because they would be profiteers.

It'll cost us less than what we're paying now. It would come out of taxes, and it would be in the government's interest to keep it economical.

That's the lesson to be learned from looking at all the other countries. All the other countries that have national health care are covered better than we are and spend less money from taxes for doing it.

• • •

I don't say that capitalism guarantees that everybody gets to be a millionaire. Guaranteeing that somebody gets to be a millionaire is a hell of a lot more wasteful and stupid than guaranteeing that everybody gets health.

• • •

Having public health care is not public assistance. It's just how we all take care of ourselves.

Public assistance means that there is a public that is separate from the government and a government that is separate from the public.

• • •

Public health care should come from the federal government, not from local governments or private groups. That would make it competitive, and I don't think health care should be competitive. At least not in the money part.

You can compete in the science part, but not the money part.

And I admit that I have this idealistic idea of science and I should probably be careful about it because it's probably naive. My idea is that you're looking for the truth and you communicate with scientists in other countries and places because you know that there's a normal distribution of intelligence throughout the species and you don't cut anybody off.

• • •

We quit building atom bombs, and we quit building B-2 bombers and all that kind of stuff. . . because if you look at the ratio of what that kind of stuff costs and what education costs, it's really a bargain to mothball all that kind of crap.

You save money and you have surplus if you knock off all of that kind of crap.

• • •

While someone is getting it together or working it out, why should their children be punished during their youthful years and conditioned in ways that they may never be able to get out from behind for the rest of their life?

We should be taking care of these children.

This is why I say in my Education Plank that every child physically present in the country should be educated, regardless of who their parents are.

And they should also have health care.

• • •

In Tennessee. . . one of our legislators is the guy who collected
$600,000 from the health care industry for proposing an alterna-
tive health care plan to Clinton's—that is, to take Clinton's out.
One of our senators is a heart surgeon and has $13 million of stock
in [Hospital Corporation of America], and his father founded
HCA, you know, and so we don't have two senators from Tennessee. One of our senators is from the Hospital Corporation of
America, and just works under Tennessee's credentials.

—Unpublished interview for *Free Spirit* magazine, with Paul English,
William Meyers, Stephany Evans, and Marc Greene, 1995